Reminders of God, Winter/Spring

Daily Inspirational Messages

Reverend Ted Rogers, Ph.D.

ISBN: 9798367635362

Contents

Dedicated to my beautiful wife, Glenda, who is light and air to me. I love her more than life.

Preface

Shortly after my ordination, I was having lunch with one of my mentors, Jim Lewis. Jim had about thirty years of pastoral ministry experience, so I asked him, "Jim, what's the biggest piece of advice you have for me as a pastor?" Jim responded instantly, "Get used to people being disappointed with you. You may be their shepherd, but they will always compare you to The Good Shepherd, and so in their estimation, they will see you at best as missing the mark." That was over thirty years ago, and Jim was correct. To survive in pastoral ministry it became clear that elephants' hide was a necessity.

Unfortunately, there has been a shift in the Church in North America that began long before that time but has gained significant velocity in the past twenty to twenty-five years, and that is this: It is no longer the pastor who needs elephants' hide to survive in the Church. No, secular politics has gained a strong foothold in Christendom, so that those who will think for themselves, instead of simply following as directed are often ostracized, and belittled, simply for trying to learn more or express a new idea.

These individuals, often those who are among the most gifted in the Church, while not giving up on their faith, do give up on what I call "churchianity." Oh, to be sure, the real Church is the amalgam of all who have placed their faith in Christ. It is the Body of Christ on earth, and of that true Body of Christ, they have no problem. Their problem, legitimately, is with those who define their "christianity" (I'm using the small "c" here on purpose) by their politics, and by a list of things they won't do, as well as by their desire to return to an imaginary utopian past, which never truly existed. These small "c" "christians," being among the most vocal group in churchianity, have no understanding of either grace (God's unmerited favor) or love.

Therefore, flocks of those who know the love of Christ, who know there is something more, leave the church. This does not mean that they cease fellowship, and certainly doesn't mean that they don't miss good, solid teaching, wherever that may be found.

I started writing these daily reminders back in 1998, in response to a very good question by one of our Church members. "Ted, what is it that God wants me to do? I just want to know that." I responded by saying "Let me rephrase that question—how about, 'What is it that God wants me to be?'" I then went on to explain how in the creation narrative, God first makes a series of domains, and He then fills those domains. For example, God creates the heavens, then He fills the heavens with light. He then separates the land from the sea, then fills each with appropriate life forms, etc. Then comes humanity.

In Genesis 1:26, we read "Then God said, 'Let Us make man in Our image, according to Our likeness; let them have dominion over the fish of the sea, over the birds of the air, and over the cattle, over all the earth and over every creeping thing that creeps on the earth.'" In studying this passage in Seminary, I was lucky to have the brilliant linguist, Dr. Ron Allen, as my instructor. Ron made the point that in virtually every translation of this passage, there is a small but significant error, in that the word translated as "in," as used in "Let us make man in our image," should be translated as "as," changing the translation then to "Let us make man as our image," (Italics mine). The historian in me resonated with this, in that in ancient empires, it was common practice for the ruler to have a statue of himself made and placed in the far outlying districts of his realm. This statue would serve to remind the inhabitants that there was a ruler, and give them a visualization of his attributes.

Applying that, then, to the enhanced, more accurate translation, The purpose of man is to serve as a reminder to all of creation that there is a God, and give the world a visualization as to the attributes of that God.

What we are to be, then is this: a reminder of God. Once we understand who we are supposed to be, it is easier for us to understand the fluidity of what we are to do as circumstances around us change.

I put that expository into an email to the congregation, who, for the most part, resonated deeply with it. Thus was born my daily writing of what I then called "Reminders of God." Each weekday for seven years I wrote and emailed out those reminders. I took a four-year break while studying for my Ph.D. comprehensive exams and writing my dissertation, but revived them shortly after that.

The unexpected result was that a following grew of those individuals who had been deeply wounded in the political abyss of North American churchianity, but who desperately wanted to hear an educated treatise on scripture that did not apply contemporary politics as its key point of hermeneutics. After several years of good friends encouraging me to put these into book form, I have finally acquiesced.

Please do not misunderstand me—There are good Churches in the US. It's just that for many, the cultural creep of a political agenda has so diluted or even inverted the message of Christ that there is a need for the teaching of scriptural truth that rejects a political agenda. This is a lacuna that I hope this work fills.

It is my sincere prayer that these words minister to you, and draw you intellectually, emotionally, and actively closer to Christ. I have used in each day's work scripture from either the New American Standard Bible, the New International Version, or the New King James translation of scripture, whichever I felt was the clearest and best for that particular passage. Often I revert to the original Greek or Hebrew to expand on key meanings in different passages.

Of course, no project like this can possibly be the work of one person. My beautiful wife of forty years, Glenda, not only offered a wellspring of encouragement but also tirelessly edited page after page. Harry Slye, my YoungLife leader of almost fifty years ago not only helped root me in my faith, but he also set an example of one who rejected the anti-intellectualism of so many in the Church and encouraged my curiosity. Also, from my high school years, Mariana Nanson not only encouraged this project but also did a very good job editing several sections. Brad Gurney, my best friend from college, has been harping on me to put these into book form for over twenty years. His friendship has been invaluable to me. Jim Lewis modeled for me what it meant to be a good pastor, as he stood out as one who loved God and understood humanity. Phil Christensen, too, is not only a great man but also a truly amazing pastor who has avoided the influx of the political into the Church. The world would be a better place if there were more pastors like him. Dr. Tom Constable, my advisor in seminary who became one of my best friends, and his wife Mary, have always encouraged Glenda and me in ministry and pushed each of us to accomplish more than we ever thought we could. And of course, my Savior, Jesus, who met me in my pain so many years ago, and who has saved me in more ways than I can count. All of these people are responsible for whatever is good in these pages. All errors and omissions are mine alone.

I pray that in these pages you see Christ anew, building that longing for the time when He will celebrate you home.

Grace, Peace, and Love,

Reverend Ted Rogers, Ph.D.

Chapter One

January

January 1

Happy New Year! The first New Year's celebration dates back over 4,000 years, but it was Julius Caesar who was the first to name it an actual Holiday, calling it "Janus" in honor of the Roman god of the same name, who had two faces, one looking forward the other looking back. This is where we get the name of the month of January. Also of interest, it was the Romans, too, who initiated ringing in the New Year with a kiss, though things tended to get even friskier back then.

Almost a full fifty percent of Americans make New Year's resolutions. As we are celebrating the start of another transit around the sun, this makes sense, as it is a means of wiping the dust of the previous year off one's feet, and choosing to move forward with life. A New Year gives us not just a sense of renewal but also reminds us that we can re-take control of our lives.

The thing is, if we treat the New Year like we did the previous year, we will see very few if any changes in our lives. For the

New Year to be meaningful, we must embrace it as both new and unique.

2 Corinthians 5:17

"Therefore, if anyone is in Christ, he is a new creation; old things have passed away; behold, all things have become new."

In Christ, we are new creations. However, if we choose to hang on to our old ideas, our old damaged senses of self-esteem, and our old habits, how are our lives going to be any different? Yes, you are a new creature, but you must choose to act on all that entails for that to transform your life.

My wife Glenda is an internationally renowned artist. She finished a painting today of a sailboat under full sail, leaning heavily with the wind. She told me, "Almost all pictures of boats I see are of a boat at a dock, on land, or at anchor. But that's not what boats were built for. I wanted to show in this a boat speeding forward not on its own power, but on a sail and jib filled with a spirited wind, dreams, and potential."

You are loved by God. In Christ, you are a completely new creation. In Christ, the old you with all of its shortcomings and hurts have passed on already.

So, are you going to let the Spirit of God fill your sails so you can reach your full potential? Or are you going to remain at the dock?

It's a New Year. You are a new creation. Just think of the potentiality in that combination!

January 2

It's funny how usually a person will signal to us who they are, yet so often we will ignore those signals, putting ourselves in harm's way. The woman who talks badly of others behind their backs? Rest assured, she's trash-talking you behind yours. The guy who is the gossip, wanting to share a "secret?" Know that he is sharing your juicy private conversations with others. People tell us who they are, but too often, we will think, "Well he/she would never do that to me, I'm his/her friend..." And every one that person is talking about thought the same thing. Never trust a gossip; never trust one who speaks badly of others behind their backs.

And never trust a tyrant.

Genghis Kahn's reputation spanned from Asia to Europe, his exploits were well known and feared by all. In 1194, Genghis Khan conquered the walled city of Tibet by promising the villagers that he would forgo any attempt to take their city by force if they would pay him the homage of 1,000 cats. The villagers knew Kahn's reputation but they acquiesced, gathering almost all of the cats kept as house pets in the city. When they turned the cats over to Khan, he instructed his troops to tie rags around the tails of the cats and light the rags aflame. The terrified kitties fled back to their respective homes, setting many of the buildings on fire. In the ensuing panic, while the people of the city tried to quench the widespread outbreak of fires, Khan's forces attacked, taking the city easily.

The villagers signed their death warrant due to their anxiety to appease.

We can let our guard down for many reasons. Sometimes we perceive no threat. Other times we may be distracted. Still, others are simply overworked and tired. Consider this:

1 Peter 5:6-8

"Humble yourselves, therefore, under the mighty hand of God, that He may exalt you at the proper time, casting all your anxiety upon Him, because He cares for you. Be of sober spirit, be on the alert. Your adversary, the devil, prowls about like a roaring lion, seeking someone to devour."

Anxieties are distractions. Cast these upon God. Humble yourself under God, trusting He will exalt you in the proper time, enabling you to focus with diligence on that which is important, and see the true nature of those around you. You know who those people are, if you're not distracted, and are paying attention, for as they prowl they roar, announcing their intent.

Stay safe!

January 3

We live in a society that abhors failure. Growing up in my family, failure, mediocrity, heck anything short of my parent's imagined idea of perfection was something to be punished. Most of Western society follows this notion that failure is to be penalized. Still, some see beyond it. I remember as a young underwriter working for an insurance company, a new hire in the commercial lines division underwrote a risk poorly, resulting in a seven-figure loss to the company. At a conference, as the individual's boss related the story, one of the attendees asked jokingly, "So where's the guy working now?" The man's boss replied, "For me. I just spent $1.7 MM to train him. I expect him to be the best and most loyal employee going forward." The room went silent.

The wise individual understands that the master of any task has failed more times than any beginner has tried. C.S. Lewis once noted, "Failures, repeated failures, are finger posts on the road to achievement. One fails forward toward success." I agree. I believe that success granted too early seduces even the smartest person into believing that they cannot lose—a lesson sure to break hearts.

Here's the money quote for the day—Each of us, every one, sometimes feels like a failure, but we need to understand failure as an event, not an identity. Again, failure is an event, not an identity. It is an event intended to teach us, to help us become better.

Psalm 37:23-24

"The steps of a good man are ordered by the Lord, And He delights in his way. Though he fall, he shall not be utterly cast down; For the Lord upholds him with His hand."

Hebrews chapter 11 is often called the "Hall of fame of faith." But let's take a look at the other side of some of those heroes mentioned. Abraham and Isaac both lied. Noah got drunk. Samson committed adultery, Gideon hid in cowardly fear, and Rahab engaged in sex for money. David committed adultery and murder, Elijah had a nervous breakdown, and Jonah ran away from God. Each of these individuals failed, but none were failures. God used them all in amazing ways.

No, though you have failed and will fail, failure is an event, NOT your identity. It means you dared to try, and hopefully to try again. Only individuals of faith fail, because only individuals of faith dare to step out to attempt to get something done. Just because you have failed, does not mean that it has become your identity. The Lord has your hand, and He's not through walking with you yet.

Have a great day! Dust yourself off, and kick it!

January 4

Renovating a house is hard. Renovating one where a portion of it is 400 years old is...interesting! The previous owners of our house in Mexico had left it vacant for about two years. Bugs, dead and alive, littered the floors, the garden was overgrown to the point it blocked the walkway and most of the central courtyard. We lost count of how many broken windows it had. The painted walls outside had oxidized and inside the walls were dirty and in many places, the plaster had cracked. The kitchen was antiquated, and the entranceway to it was so low I had to duck to get in.

Six months of work, six days a week...

And it had to be done in the proper order. First, we fumigated to kill all the critters. This meant leaving it vacant for two days for the insecticide to disperse. Then there was the water system. In Mexico, each house has its own water pressure system, and most of them are inadequate and erratic. We had to pull out the old quarter-inch pipe and upgrade to ¾-inch pipe, which meant tearing into the masonry walls, then re-cementing after all was done. We tackled the garden and the kitchen at the same time, upgraded the wiring, and brought new life into the 200-year-old fountain. Finally, painting took a professional crew well over a month to complete.

85% of our budget we spent on infrastructure improvements that are invisible to the naked eye but made the house livable. Then and only then, it was time for powder and rouge...

Unfortunately, in our relationship with God, we tend to ignore the infrastructure, and go straight for the powder and rouge...

Romans 12:11-12

"Never be lacking in zeal, but keep your spiritual fervor, serving the Lord. Be joyful in hope, patient in affliction, faithful in prayer.

Psalm 119:15

"I meditate on your precepts and consider your ways."

Romans 10:17

"Consequently, faith comes from hearing the message, and the message is heard through the word about Christ."

Many individuals are at Church whenever the door is open, but that does not make one a Christian, just like sitting in one's garage does not make a person a car. And then there's the lingo, the Christianese that sets one apart to look/sound spiritual, and utterly turns the stomachs of those who are outside of the Church... "Have a blessed day," instead of "Have a good day" and "Let go and let God," instead of "Chill." The list goes on.

Now maybe, just maybe, some of these things are legit, but they look an awful lot like powder and rouge when God is concerned with our infrastructure, and building our infrastructure comes from prayer, talking to God, meditation, which is thoughtfully listening to God, and reading God's love letter—Scripture. When those three things are in place, a radical dynamic takes place. We grow in God's love, which pushes us into the world to love it and serve it. We then face troubling things, which pushes us back into prayer, meditation, and study of scripture, which again pushes us out into the world, to love and serve.

Or we can just pay the pastor to study and pray for us, and show up on Sunday morning to have him tell us what to do, even though our spiritual infrastructure, our relationship with God, is corrupted or non-existent.

Because the reality is that one can never delegate a relationship.

Gotta run, someone I need to talk to...

January 5

I LOVED the movie Second Hand Lions. Such a sweet, compassionate film. Two of the heroes of the movie, the uncles of a young boy with a TERRIBLE mother, purchase an aged lion that they intend to hunt on their ranch. But the boy, instead, makes a pet out of the lion. The movie revolves around the boy and his uncles making peace with one another and building in the end a truly loving familial relationship.

While one may be able to buy a previously owned lion, there is no "used" Jesus, no secondhand Savior.

More than I care to admit, I've inherited my father's sometimes acerbic nature. Glenda, fortunately, inherited her grandmother's sweet, kind spirit. But some things you just can't inherit. Too often I'll be talking to someone, and they'll say something like "Of course I'm a Christian, I mean I'm not Jewish or Buddhist. I mean, my family has been a member of the (fill in the denomination of your choice) for generations." So sorry, but what this person is describing is, at best, a relationship with a denomination, not a relationship with the Church, and certainly not a relationship with Christ.

Then there's the "I was born into a Christian family, and have been a Christian all my life..."

Utterly impossible, and I cringe when I hear that, knowing that a legalist is standing right in front of me.

Consider these words:

1 John 5:11-12

"And this is the testimony: God has given us eternal life, and this life is in his Son. Whoever has the Son has life; whoever does not have the Son of God does not have life."

The Greek word here translated as "has" means literally, "to hold, to hold on to." It is indicative of an individual action to successfully grab ahold of something or someone.

It denotes an individual, not a corporate act. No one can do it for you. Your grasp of something or someone cannot be inherited.

It must be your choice.

I honestly believe that the most important question one can ask of themselves is if they have made the personal choice to grab ahold of Christ. Not the Churchianity version, not the Cosmic Killjoy, but the God of Love, who enjoyed wine, hung around with a rough crowd, and made the Churchianity types of his day uncomfortable (the real Christ still does today).

Maybe your parents or grandparents were people of faith. Maybe you're a member of a denomination.

But there is no such thing as a secondhand Savior.

Aslan would not like that idea!

Take the time to ponder...

January 6

At the time of Jesus' coming, The Roman Empire dominated the nation of Israel in a brutal occupation. The people of Israel prayed actively for the coming of the promised Messiah. They wanted a liberator to help them cast off the political and military dominance of Rome.

The term "Messiah" can have two meanings. The first is "Liberator." The second is "Savior." The term liberator was how the Israelites understood the meaning of Messiah, and they sought liberation in both the political and military sense.

Then came Jesus...

Jesus was apolitical.

Jesus was the Prince of Peace.

Jesus was not the Messiah they had desired.

Think on this: in Jesus' closest group, he included a tax collector—a collaborator with the Roman government, who was therefore thought of as a traitor to Israel. He also chose a Zealot—A member of a sect intent on the violent overthrow of Rome.

While the Israelites wanted a political Messiah, Jesus instead came as the Christ—meaning literally "the anointed one to his great redemptive work as Prophet, Priest, and King of his people." Savior, but not in the political, worldly sense, instead, the one who would bridge the gap between God and man. In His own words, of His mission on earth, here is what He said:

John 6:51

"I am the living bread which came down from heaven. If anyone eats of this bread, he will live forever; and the bread that I shall give is My flesh, which I shall give for the life of the world."

In other words, Jesus came to give His life so that anyone choosing to accept that would have true and eternal life.

We humans are poor historians for the most part. For the past twenty-five or so years, I have seen a HUGE segment of the "Church" in North America forget the real reason why Jesus came, and instead attempt to force the idea of Jesus into a political mold. Perhaps it is just easier to have voted for a legislator to attempt change through political means than for the Church to take up its real job, and be the Body of Christ on earth, feeding the poor, giving to those who ask, welcoming the immigrant, loving our neighbors as ourselves, even if they look or believe differently.

Jesus chose which definition of Messiah He wanted to apply. As "Christians," or, literally, "little Christs," shouldn't we follow in His footsteps?

January 7

Sacrifice. By its nature, a sacrifice costs us something. Sacrifice is a real part of life, especially a life lived with passion. As John Galsworthy noted in the early 1900s, "The value of a sentiment is the amount of sacrifice you are prepared to make for it." So true. Talk can be cheap—how are we prepared to live our lives, and what are we willing to sacrifice to do it—that's the question!

Scripture speaks of bringing to God a "sacrifice of praise." For years that had me stumped, then in a season of melancholy, I understood what the writer meant. Irrespective of my circumstances, or my sadness, God had not changed. He was still majestic, still loving, still awesome. God transcends circumstance, and we owe Him our praise by virtue of His very nature. It is in those times of melancholy that it is a sacrifice to lift our eyes from our circumstances, and praise God for who He is.

Hebrews 13:15-16

"Through Jesus, therefore, let us continually offer to God a sacrifice of praise—the fruit of lips that confess his name. And do not forget to do good and to share with others, for with such sacrifices God is pleased."

Funny thing--I have found that in those dark times when I have brought a sacrifice of praise to God, in looking on Him, in thinking about who He is, how He transcends events no matter how dark, my perspective changed, and I, too, was able to rise above the circumstance, in God's power.

January 8

"Seriously, would you pay 5,000 pesos for THAT?" A person ripped into Glenda about one of her paintings. A very accomplished artist standing next to Glenda said "I sure would!" The critic, who had never made a work of art himself, left. Similarly, I've had three people massively criticize my first book. The first one never even bothered to read it, just cut into the title. The other two had no understanding of the history or personalities I had written about—they had just made up their minds from pop culture representations of the individuals featured. And none of them had any work of theirs published. My point is this—It is a bankable statement that 99.9% of those who criticize you have accomplished far less than you. Pause, think back on the most stinging critiques you've received—It's true, isn't it!?!

Teddy Roosevelt understood this when he penned a quote that has helped me through many a tough time "It is not the critic who counts; not the man who points out how the strong man stumbles, or where the doer of deeds could have done them better. The credit belongs to the man who is actually in the arena, whose face is marred by dust and sweat and blood, who strives valiantly; who errs and comes short again and again; because there is no effort without error and shortcomings; but who does actually strive to do the deed; who knows the great enthusiasm, the great devotion, who spends himself in a worthy cause, who at the best knows, in the end, the triumph of high achievement and who at the worst, if he fails, at least he fails while daring greatly. So that his place shall never be with those cold and timid souls who know neither victory nor defeat."

And oh, my friend, this world is filled with cold, timid souls...

Matthew 25:14-26

"Again, it will be like a man going on a journey, who called his servants and entrusted his wealth to them. To one he gave five bags of gold, to another two bags, and to another one bag, each according to his ability. Then he went on his journey. The man who had received five bags of gold went at once and put his money to work and gained five bags more. So also, the one with two bags of gold gained two more. But the man who had received one bag went off, dug a hole in the ground and hid his master's money. "After a long time the master of those servants returned and settled accounts with them. The man who had received five bags of gold brought the other five. 'Master,' he said, 'you entrusted me with five bags of gold. See, I have gained five more.' "His master replied, 'Well done, good and faithful servant! You have been faithful with a few things; I will put you in charge of many things. Come and share your master's happiness!' "The man with two bags of gold also came. 'Master,' he said, 'you entrusted me with two bags of gold; see, I have gained two more.' "His master replied, 'Well done, good and faithful servant! You have been faithful with a few things; I will put you in charge of many things. Come and share your master's happiness!'

"Then the man who had received one bag of gold came. 'Master,' he said, 'I knew that you are a hard man, harvesting where you have not sown and gathering where you have not scattered seed. So I was afraid and went out and hid your gold in the ground. See, here is what belongs to you.' "His master replied, 'You wicked, lazy servant! So you knew that I harvest where I have not sown and gather where I have not scattered seed? Well then, you should have put my money on deposit with the bankers, so that when I returned I would have received it back with interest."

One could write a dissertation on this passage, but an oft-overlooked application is that whether the servant earned five bags of gold or two, the reward and praise were the same. It was only the servant who did nothing who received not just criticism, but a rebuke from his master.

There are battles ahead of you. Fight. You may be in an arena with others watching—pay them no heed, Fight. Your face may be marred with sweat and blood, Fight. You will at times fail, err. Fight. And when all is said and done, you will stand, and enter into the joy of your master.

The referee is about to hit the bell. Come out swinging, and pay no attention to the critic, who just buries his or her talent.

Fight.

January 9

At night, before we go to bed, my wife and I read children's stories to each other. Ok, truth be told, she usually reads to me, but after a long day of dealing with adult issues, the joy and innocence of James and the Giant Peach, or The Trumpet of the Swan, is both seductive and soothing. As well, the stories prove to be reminders of life lessons we as adults often forget.

Here's an example: the story of Beauty and the Beast is on many plains terrifying—to the degree that I've often wondered if it was appropriate for young children! Yet there is a significant life lesson to take from the story, and that is, as G.K. Chesterton noted, that a person must first be loved before they can become loveable.

1 John 4:19-21

"We love, because He first loved us. If someone says, "I love God," and yet he hates his brother or sister, he is a liar; for the one who does not love his brother and sister whom he has seen, cannot love God, whom he has not seen. And this commandment we have from Him, that the one who loves God must also love his brother and sister."

G.K. Chesterton was both a literary master and an insightful critic. In 1911, Chesterton wrote about the works of Charles Dickens, Chesterton wisely noting that "The whole difference between construction and creation is exactly this: that a thing constructed can only be loved after it is constructed; but a thing created is loved before it exists, as the mother can love the unborn child." Wow, "Loved before it exists..."

And God loved you my friend before your birth.

This makes you loveable beyond measure.

Yes, we love because God first loved us. Now, in our state of being both loved and loveable, we must go out into the world, not in judgment or condemnation, but in love.

In doing so we will see the transformative effects on our society as God's love is lived out in and through us.

I hope you have a great day and know that you are both loved, and loveable.

January 10

I like Octopuses. When Glenda and I were in Grenada, we were sitting on a dock, dangling our feet in the ocean, and a school of baby octopuses came over to Glenda and played with her. They are the smartest of any invertebrate. They have three hearts, blue blood, and see not only with their arms but also with their skin. Also, a 600-pound octopus can squeeze through a tube the diameter of a quarter. WHAT!! Yuppers. A 600-pound octopus can navigate its way through a tube the diameter of a quarter.

Why can't you do that? Simple.

You have a spine.

That is also what allows you to walk upright, like a real human. Too bad so many, often those in leadership roles, don't seem to remember they have a spine...

2 Timothy 1:6-7

"For this reason I remind you to kindle afresh the gift of God which is in you through the laying on of my hands. For God has not given us a spirit of timidity, but of power and love and discipline."

I've seen a great deal of upsetting things this past week. And contributing to that are the individuals who are so concerned with pleasing others that they do nothing to try to please God. They claim Christ but are so vacuously timid in standing up for the truth that it is hard to take their profession of faith seriously. Their desire to fit in transcends any connection they have with the truth.

And that is not from God.

God does not give us a spirit of timidity, but of power—That is the strength to do the right thing. He also gives us the spirit of Love—that is, the ability to temper our actions with compassion. And He gives us the Spirit of discipline—in part, the rationale to be sure that what we are speaking is the truth, to check the facts, instead of just going with our ideologies or the ideologies of our "friends."

You have a spine. You have the Spirit of power, Love, and discipline.

So stand up, and use them regularly, and you will change the world.

January 11

I love how God designed even nature to be a community. The rain doesn't fall for its own benefit, but it waters the plants and fills the streams. The stream flows not of selfish ambition, but as a home to fish and frogs, and it waters the tree. The tree grows not for its glory, but to provide food for others, a nesting place for birds, and shade for the weary traveler. And so on. God designed nature and humanity to work together in a sense of community.

And yet, so often, we choose to treat life as a zero-sum game, which wipes out any possibility of community.

It's been said, "No man is an island unto himself." I disagree. Thinking of an old friend from some 40 years back, a thoughtful, gentle man then. Yet somehow he bought into the zero-sum game mentality regarding life. Oh, he has prospered materially, yet he has lost multiple wives, in that marriage was also a zero-sum game, and he is cranky, grumpy, and bitter, in his seven-figure home, all alone.

In the New Testament, we see the importance of community as a relentlessly repeated trope. The phrase "One another" factors in 100 times. Though individuals fully and unique, we are intended to stand and work together.

1 Corinthians 12:20-27

"But now indeed there are many members, yet one body. And the eye cannot say to the hand, "I have no need of you"; nor again the head to the feet, "I do not need of you." No, much rather, those members of the body which seem to be weaker are necessary. And those members of the body which we think to be less honorable, on these we bestow greater honor; and our unpresentable parts have greater modesty, but our presentable parts have no need. But God composed the body, having given greater honor to that part which lacks it, that there should be no schism in the body, but that the members should have the same care for one another. And if one member suffers, all the members suffer with it; or if one member is honored, all the members rejoice with it. Now you are the body of Christ, and members individually."

One of the things I love about living in Mexico is the sense of community. One of my best buddies here runs a touring company. When he leads his tours, as able, he splits the group up for lunches, so that he can help distribute the commerce among different vendors in an attempt to build a healthy community. Community is not about geography, but about care and inclusiveness. The idea of an exclusive community is oxymoronic. As Anatol Rapaport noted, "The moral development of civilization is measured by the breadth of its sense of community." We need each other, working together, to advance.

My wife is out of town, and I feel as if I have a hole in the core of my being because I do not live for myself, but for her. And for you. And for my neighbors. And for my pups. Take any away, my very being is diminished. If I were to live for myself, oh how very boring, bitter, and besieged I would be!

Think on it this way: community is where the best part of humanity and the Glory of God meet together to create that which is greater than the sum of its parts, so use your gifts! You don't have to be perfect! The forest would be a very quiet place if only the perfect bird sang!

My challenge to you is this—As you walk down the corridor at work, or down the street, smile at the grump, call them by name, and wish them a good day. In doing so you are inviting them into your community. And they may be a grump. But like the erosive power of water, the erosive power of love eats away at the walls people build around their hearts.

And when betting on rock or water, remember water always wins...

January 12

The average person in Mexico makes about $100.00 per week, as of the time of this writing. And yet, Mexico is the second happiest country in the world. As I write this, I'm listening to the mechanic working next door, Beating a crumpled car door back into shape with a hammer, singing loudly, with every hammer strike in time to the music. And he laughs. I once interned at one of the wealthiest churches in the United States. "Joy" and "happiness" were concepts seldom seen. The magazine "Texas Monthly" quoted one of the pastoral staff members as saying that the unofficial motto of the Church was "Love things, use people." I think he was spot on...about that Church, and many others, unfortunately!

At the start of the COVID crisis, an artist friend began doing online auctions of his work to make money to give to those in need. He told me that time and again, as he went to families he knew required assistance, they would more often than not decline his offer of food, telling him instead of where someone with greater need lived, so he could take the gift to them instead. Those same families would scrape up their last centavos, too, to purchase kibble for the stray street dogs, so they did not starve.

Back in the States, I found it most common in the Church that individuals sought gifts, instead of seeking to build a relationship with the gift giver, God. In great part, I think the reason why is that worry, especially worry over material things, is a systemic problem in our culture.

Matthew 6:25-27

"Therefore I say to you, do not worry about your life, what you will eat or what you will drink; nor about your body, what you will put on. Is not life more than food and the body more than clothing? Look at the birds of the air, for they neither sow nor reap nor gather into barns; yet your heavenly Father feeds them. Are you not of more value than they? Which of you by worrying can add one cubit to his stature?"

When I worked as a financial analyst at EDS, I was brought into the Executive Development Program, which was a stepping-stone to upper management. The leader of the program instructed us that for our best employees, we should encourage them to purchase homes WAY beyond their price range, as the fear they would then have would keep them locked into the company—oh, and too, with that, we were to increase their workloads so they wouldn't have time to look elsewhere for work. "Dress for the job you want, not the job you have…"

And no one was content.

And that is utterly counter to God's plan.

Consistently I have seen that those who have the least are going to be the ones who, percentage-wise, give the most. And they are storing up treasure in heaven, while oh so many others are bankrupt—morally and spiritually. As G.K. Chesterton noted, "There are two ways to get enough. One is to continue to accumulate more and more. The other is to desire less." Wise words that fly in the face of most of our culture.

There is happiness, not shame, in simplifying our lives. There is joy in giving. But until we are satisfied with knowing the gift giver, instead of seeking the material gifts, we will be hard-pressed to experience that.

Pause, look up instead of out, and seek the deeper relationship. You will find contentment flows with the Spirit of God.

January 13

Ahhh, the sin sniffers! What a fun lot! They seem to be self-appointed bloodhounds, on scent for any bit of sin (in others, of course) that they can find. Evidently, by putting others down, they mistakenly feel they can walk across those sinners' backs to lift themselves closer to God. About a year ago I had a former parishioner tell me that whenever she sees sin, she has to "call it out." My thought was "Sweet pea, then how can you ever leave the mirror in the morning..."

Individuals like this always have their go-to verse, and usually, that is 1 Thessalonians 5:22. In the King James Version, it reads, "Avoid every appearance of evil." Now, first, the King James translation could be considered at best a reasonably good first try at translating scripture from Hebrew and Greek to English. But the scholarship was lacking, and the English is now archaic, as meanings for certain words have drifted over time. No, most contemporary translations read something like "Abstain from every form of evil..." But even there the scholarship often takes a backseat to the political issues of translation. Let's look more into the context.

1 Thessalonians 5:21-23

"Test all things; hold fast what is good. Abstain from every form of evil. Now may the God of peace Himself sanctify you completely; and may your whole spirit, soul, and body be preserved blameless at the coming of our Lord Jesus Christ."

The word translated here as "evil" is the noun "eidos," which meant literally "mint" (as in coinage). Now here is where historian Ted meets theologian Ted. A phrase attributed to Christ in extra-biblical literature is very similar, reading "become approved money-changers by abstaining from evil things and holding fast to what is good." If this is so, then Paul, while writing to the Church in Thesolonica, was actually quoting Christ, effectively saying, "Test all things! Make sure you don't pass on any fake coins!" Thus, applying a good hermeneutic, it means to avoid passing on false doctrines. As Paul then goes on to say "may the God of peace Himself sanctify you completely..." This reminds us that the work of sanctification, that is, making us holy, is the responsibility of God.

That kind of takes a bit of weight off of one, huh?

There is an inherent problem with the sin sniffers. In taking on the mantel of judge, they are assuming a right claimed by God as His and his alone. In claiming then to be like God, they are acting in the role of Satan. If they are simply accusing, not judging, then again, Satan has the role of accuser, and they are then uniting themselves with him.

But God offers love. But God does the work of sanctification in our lives, as we cannot do it. But God accepts us as we are. So Paul here is saying, in light of all God has done and is doing, let's not muddy the waters with crap doctrine.

I hope this brings you some peace and serves in some way as an antidote to the guilt trips given by others. And, too, I hope that you know that you are loved.

January 14

As I write this, my wife, aka the "Wild Love Monkey" is in the kitchen making soap. It's a fairly complicated process involving goats' milk, coconut oil, olive oil, essential oils, and lye, all organic. The lye makes the process dangerous, as lye can burn one's skin, direct contact or fumes can permanently burn one's eyes, and the fumes can cause massive lung damage. In fact, the lye is so caustic that one cannot even use the soap for 30 days after it is made.

You see, as the soap ages, the lye interacts with the other ingredients. Those ingredients work to neutralize the pH of the lye, so that, after time, it is actually mild and not just useful for cleansing, but also good for moisturizing the skin

That's right—what would cause burns and blisters today can bring cleansing and healing after it has aged a bit.

But we live in an instant culture. We want what we want when we want it, and that goes for the machinations of our own lives as well. We recognize our faults, at least on an unconscious level, though those more self-actualized see them on the higher planes. And oh so often we are quick to chastise ourselves, punish ourselves even, no matter how small the fault in question. Hey, which of us hasn't done something like look for our glasses when they are on top of our head, or used the flashlight of your cell phone to try to find ...your cell phone? And we feel doltish, though we try to laugh it off. But deep inside there is that niggling question "When will I be good enough...when will I start to act like a grownup..." And the more caustic our failings, the deeper our self-criticism.

Philippians 2:13-16a

"For it is God who works in you to will and to act in order to fulfill his good purpose. Do everything without grumbling or arguing, so that you may become blameless and pure, children of God without fault in a warped and crooked generation. Then you will shine among them like stars in the sky as you hold firmly to the word of life."

Yes, like the lye in soap, there is a caustic nature in all of us. All of us can, and have burned and blistered others.

But...

When we internalize Christ, accept His gift of not just forgiveness, but of adoption, He begins to work in us, transforming our caustic nature, exorcising the darkness, so that we will shine like stars in the sky.

And yet we want what we want when we want it because our culture has trained us to see and understand events, and not processes. But God's work in you is a process, the instilling of a metamorphosis. It is called sanctification, which means being made "holy" which simply means being set aside to God and His loving purpose, as opposed to the harshness of this world.

And He does the work, giving us nothing to boast about except for His presence in us.

Oh, and know this—I see the light in you...

January 15

My morning time with my double espresso is sacred! Oh, that velvety dark brew, with a hint of cocoa flavor on the back taste... And this morning, I was just putting the demitasse cup to my lips, inhaling the aroma, when our puppy, Chaucer Chaucer Puppy Bosser came loping around the corner and clipped me on both knees. Espresso flew in the air, as I watched it all happen in slow motion. Some went up my nose, some onto my face, but most…most went onto my shirt. The dark brown liquid was first hot, then rapidly became cool. Now, the cup was still intact, but… "Darn!" I said (If you believe that, well, I have some property to sell you…).

Now the thing is, though Chaucer caused the spill, it wasn't his fault that it was espresso that spilled. Espresso was in the cup. It could have been milk, tea, scotch (well, it was a bit early for scotch), you name it. The point is, and I wish I could credit the person who first said this, but I can't find the quote, whatever filled the cup is what was going to spill.

And life is sometimes like that; you're getting ready to take a draught and BLAM! Something hits you, and the emotional content of your life spills forth.

Ephesians 3:14-19

"For this reason I bow my knees to the Father of our Lord Jesus Christ, from whom the whole family in heaven and earth is named, that He would grant you, according to the riches of His glory, to be strengthened with might through His Spirit in the inner man, that Christ may dwell in your hearts through faith; that you, being rooted and grounded in love, may be able to comprehend with all the saints what is the width and length and depth and height—to know the love of Christ which passes knowledge; that you may be filled with all the fullness of God."

We may think we know the content of our heart, but when life hits us, well, what's in there spills out, sometimes leaving a stain. It may be anger, depression, insecurity, impatience, or the fullness of the love of God.

My point is, that what fills our hearts is, in the end, our choice. Typically, what one immerses themselves in is what fills us.

And the world calls with so many distractions in which we choose to swim...

But then there is Love. Then there is God, in all His fullness. And we have a choice.

Spills will happen. The content of those spills is up to us.

January 16

I LOVE fountain pens, and those of you who know me know that I have a large collection of them...which makes absolutely NO sense, as those of you who know me well also have seen my TERRIBLE handwriting. It's always been bad. Back in grade school though, what I got busted for the most was margins. Yuppers, I was the kid who would squeeze as many words into that forbidden one-inch space as possible.

Margins. Do you know why they exist? I mean, they're not cost-effective when you think about it! Here's the deal:

While rats are highly intelligent, rats cannot read (well, there is a bipedal form that can, but...). Yet rats DO like paper—especially to eat it. Back in the 1800s, periodicals and blank writing paper were shipped by boat and by rail. The time-consuming journeys allowed rats the opportunity to eat the paper. The publishers and paper manufacturers wanted to make sure that their customers could still use or read their products, so they added margins.

Ahh, margins. I still screw them up, except now I am adept at screwing them up in my life. I am terrible about boundaries, and simply try to do too much, allowing the urgent to crowd out my time to act upon what is actually important. And then there are the rats that eat away at those margins...

Psalm 46:9-11

"He makes wars cease to the end of the earth; He breaks the bow and cuts the spear in two; He burns the chariot in the fire.

Be still, and know that I am God; I will be exalted among the nations, I will be exalted in the earth!

The Lord of hosts is with us;

The God of Jacob is our refuge. Selah"

"Be still and know that I am God." You see God intended us to have times of stillness.

He intends us to have margins.

He knows there are rats out there.

When I was eighteen, I spent a summer working at a YoungLife camp in Colorado. Behind the dorm was a large hill, with a stone ledge on the backside of it overlooking the forest. Someone had chiseled into the stone "Be still, and know that I am God." The memory of sitting on that bare ledge reading those words has saved my life more than once.

God not only gives us permission to be still, but the verb tense used here is also the imperative: it is a command. For we cannot hear, understand, or fellowship with God if we allow mayhem to rule at the throne of our life.

As I write this, it is mid-week, and if you are like me, the urgent calls and we are tempted to ignore that which is important. But be still. Know that He is God. And let His peace, His love, His priorities back into your life.

And also know that some crazy guy in Mexico thinks you're pretty cool and hopes you have a great day.

January 17

About two weeks ago, a friend posted a question on Facebook: "Did any of you follow your childhood dreams? Are you doing now what you wanted to do then?" The answers made me want to cry, for not a single of the over 100 respondents was living their dream. The response that hit me the hardest was this: "I wanted to be a dancer. From my early childhood through high school, I took dance lessons every week. Tap, ballet, modern, and I won several awards. When I was starting college, my parents told me I was not allowed to major or minor in dance. I had to choose something practical, something normal. It broke my spirit so much that since I started at the university some thirty years ago, I have not danced again, not even at a party with my date." In almost every single answer, the different individuals bemoaned having abandoned their dreams for security, normalcy, and safety.

Every three-year-old, every six-year-old is a visionary. Yet by their mid-twenties, most people are fighting tooth and nail to excel at normalcy, to take the safe path, vision be damned.

And yet, I contend that if we claim to worship a God who is in every aspect from Love, to power, to gentleness, to creativity, and more, to live a life of normalcy dishonors the extraordinary God.

And the reasons are varied…

"I'm afraid I won't be loved."

Romans 8:38-39—"For I am convinced that neither death, nor life, nor angels, nor principalities, nor things present, nor things to come, nor powers, nor height, nor depth, nor any other created thing will be able to separate us from the love of God that is in Christ Jesus our Lord."

"I don't want to be left."

Hebrews 13:5 "Make sure that your character is free from the love of money, being content with what you have; for

He Himself has said, "I will never desert you, nor will I ever abandon you,"

"I don't have what it takes"

Isaiah 58:11 "And the Lord will continually guide you, and satisfy your desire in scorched places, and give strength to your bones; and you will be like a watered garden, and like a spring of water whose waters do not fail."

And the list goes on…

So here is my question: If you honestly believe that nothing can separate us from the love of God, not even our failures, if you truly understand that the God of the universe will never leave you, never forsake you, what, then really, do you want to do with your life?

Time to start planning.

January 18

The GREAT LIE, which has caused more guilt, and driven more people FROM God than virtually any other (Now hear this in a sweet Southern accent) "Honey, God will never give you anything more than you can handle…"

Baloney!!!!

Tell that to the woman just diagnosed with breast cancer. Tell that load of excrement to the child whose parents just told him they had him for tax reasons. Tell that to the rape victim, the woman who just miscarried, the man who lost his wife and child in a car wreck.

And it adds to their misery a ton of guilt because the person saying it was too damn lazy or scared to get in, get dirty, and help. Platitudes are nothing but cold comfort.

Here's some truth for you:

2 Corinthians 2, 1:8-9

"We do not want you to be uninformed, brothers and sisters, about the troubles we experienced in the province of Asia. We were under great pressure, far beyond our ability to endure, so that we despaired of life itself. Indeed, we felt we had received the sentence of death. But this happened that we might not rely on ourselves but on God, who raises the dead."

SCREW the GUILT TRIPS! Yes, God does allow things to hit us that are beyond us, no matter what the legalists say! And they burn us, break us, and in the breaking, a bit of light seeps in. And in the crucifixion, the battering, some, outside, see in our brokenness, grace. And in the Hell, some see Christ, as He sustains us.

"God never shuts a door without opening a window" What is that supposed to mean? As a Christian, my friend, you will be broken. Sometimes in little chips, sometimes in large slabs. God never intends for you to jump out of some window...

There was a rectangle in Tuscany of marble. First-tier, the best of marble. The rectangle of marble was beautiful. But then Michelangelo appeared and began hacking at first large chunks, then smaller chips of the stone away, to create the great statue of David. In other words, he chipped away to remove everything that wasn't art.

Friend, that is how God deals with us. Anyone saying anything else is selling something, usually just cheap grace.

If you are in the process of being broken, don't let ANYONE guilt trip you. And know that God's love for you still stands.

Crucified with Christ...That's personally identifying with the pain and love of God. Broken. Well that's where the light gets in

I pray you are well. But if you are not, remember as Maya Angelou noted, "Every storm runs out of rain."

And know this: You.Are.Loved.

January 19

I'm tired and just finished working on my Spanish for the past half hour. I do this daily and have for the past 887 days without missing a day. It is important to me, in that I am an immigrant, A US citizen who now resides in Mexico with Residente Permanente status—The Mexican government graciously extended to Glenda and me all of the rights and privileges of a citizen, except for the right to vote. The community here has embraced us, and about half of the friends we have made are Mexican nationals. As such, we are both working very hard to learn the language of the land, so that we can communicate without others having to work hard to understand us.

There are so very many boundaries in this world. Some of the physical, others cultural, some political, still others linguistic...the list goes on. And yet here is the deal: boundaries exist to be crossed, and in the process of crossing, we find that our lives are changed, and that we become change agents.

Galatians 3: 26-29

"So in Christ Jesus you are all children of God through faith, for all of you who were baptized into Christ have clothed yourselves with Christ. There is neither Jew nor Gentile, neither slave nor free, nor is there male and female, for you are all one in Christ Jesus. If you belong to Christ, then you are Abraham's seed, and heirs according to the promise."

There is the Residente Permanente visa, and there are the Residente Temporal (temporary resident) statuses. Too, there is the tourist visa, which is basically "just passing through." Here's something to consider—If, in Christ, our citizenship is now in heaven, we all must then acknowledge that we do not have a Residente Permanente visa here on earth, but instead it is Residente Temporal. Our time here is limited. So what are we going to do with it?

What is the language we must learn to get by, to be the change agent, living across the boundary from our true home? That, my friends, is the language of Love. The language that allows us to rejoice with those who rejoice, weep with those who weep, and live in harmony with one another.

There is an edge to a life in Christ, and that is knowing and understanding the idea of where our true citizenship lay, but then also acknowledging that we are foreigners in a strange land, so we must learn the language if we are to be effective.

And that means looking past differences.

And that means accepting others where they are, as they are.

Just like Christ accepted you.

January 20

Oh, how we like to think of life as a binary! "It is this or that, 0 or 1, yes or no." So often this binary thinking causes us to see life as a series of events, rather than a process. In so doing, we lose our appreciation for seasonality and become blind to the interconnectedness of life. Consider this story:

John 8:2-11

"Now early in the morning He came again into the temple, and all the people came to Him; and He sat down and taught them. Then the scribes and Pharisees brought to Him a woman caught in adultery. And when they had set her in the midst, they said to Him, "Teacher, this woman was caught in adultery, in the very act. Now Moses, in the law, commanded us that such should be stoned. But what do You say?" This they said, testing Him, that they might have something of which to accuse Him. But Jesus stooped down and wrote on the ground with His finger, as though He did not hear.

So when they continued asking Him, He raised Himself up and said to them, "He who is without sin among you, let him throw a stone at her first." And again He stooped down and wrote on the ground.

Then those who heard it, being convicted by their conscience, went out one by one, beginning with the oldest even to the last. And Jesus was left alone, and the woman standing in the midst. When Jesus had raised Himself up and saw no one but the woman, He said to her, "Woman, where are those accusers of yours? Has no one condemned you?"

She said, "No one, Lord."

And Jesus said to her, "Neither do I condemn you; go and sin no more."

There is so much here, not even touching on the fact that the man the woman had been with was not brought out with her. But think on this. We know that "sin" is falling short of the glory of God—It is a nature, not an act. Jesus tells this woman who must be terrified that he does not condemn her. Then He goes further, and tells her to do the impossible "go and sin no more." What's going on?

In doing this, Jesus is giving her the gift of forgiveness, but also letting her know that her need for Him, though immediate at that moment, will not end. She cannot, just as all of us cannot, "go and sin no more." Her need for Christ would continue. Yes, there was an event of forgiveness, but that started an ongoing process of relying on Christ.

It is so easy to point to an event in a stadium or Church, and point back some many years ago to a profession of faith made and say, "I was saved then." The reality is, when asked if one is saved, a proper response could be "I was, I am, and I hope to be." Because yes, there is an event many can point to, but that is just the beginning of a process, of a relationship that exists now, and will grow even more in the future.

Christ simply was saying to this woman that her need for Him was ongoing.

As is our need for Christ.

January 21

It is an odd feeling having just turned sixty this year. It seems like yesterday that Glenda and I were dating, just a moment ago that I was defending my dissertation, and just an hour ago that I hugged Millie the Wonderdog, who left for the Rainbow Bridge years ago. It is so weird how oh so often though the days may seem to drag, the years fly by.

And I so regret having wasted any precious second. The idiocy of looking at pictures of cute puppies on Instagram, while my beautiful dogs are at my feet, wanting a loving hand on their heads, the times spent in spurious arguments over issues of nonsense—Those choices are choices not to live, but instead to waste a portion of ones' life.

Ephesians 5:15-16

"See then that you walk circumspectly, not as fools but as wise, redeeming the time, because the days are evil."

The word translated here as "redeeming" is the Greek word "exagerazo," with a literal meaning of "To buy up, to ransom." It involves a decision, as in a choice to spurn one thing, in order to invest in something else.

Redeeming the time...taking the option to live in a manner that has meaning, to spurn the culture of time-wasting to abide with, and create significance.

Every minute wasted is a minute of life gone. A minute that could be spent building another person up, a minute that might make a sad person smile. A minute in an embrace, a kiss...

It is the natural order of this world to seek to waste our time. We can make the conscious decision, instead, to make meaning, beauty, and love, with the moments we have.

January 22

Ahhh, art! Without art, earth would just be "eh"! Whether it is the art of the storyteller writing a book, the painter, the dancer, or the musician, you name it, art brings joy, depth, and meaning to the world.

We are hardwired to understand life through stories. So much so that even when we sleep, our brains tell us stories through dreams. Glenda and I are re-reading Slaughterhouse-Five right now. It, To Kill a Mockingbird, and Catcher in the Rye are probably my three favorite books.

The thing is, as both Glenda and I are published authors, we know the publishing industry well. We have each interacted with major agents as well as publishing house executives who say matter-of-factly, with no regret, that neither of the three books I mentioned would probably be published today if they came out as new. Agents and publishing houses USED to be the gatekeepers for the industry to make sure that only the best quality literature was published. There are still many good agents and publishers, but now, many focus only on the bottom line—Pushing what will sell the quickest instead of what is the best.

The result is this: some of the best books ever written are likely never published. Writing a book is hard work. Then the expense of content editing, grammar editing, book cover design, and the book hasn't even been presented to an agent yet. Then there is the rejection process of sending out the queries to the agents. Gone With the Wind was rejected by over 40 publishers, and A Wrinkle in Time was rejected over 25 times. Life of Pi was rejected so often that the author almost gave up, until it was picked up by a small publisher in Canada.

The fact is most authors quit pushing their book before it is ever published. And for those who do get published, the vast majority then do nothing to market their work. And so the likelihood is that the "Great American Novel" has probably already been written, and is shelved on an old hard drive somewhere.

Unfortunately today, often the Church acts like many of the contemporary agents or publishing houses. "ministry belongs in the hands of the professionals," is too often the message.

Matthew 5:14-16

"You are the light of the world. A city that is set on a hill cannot be hidden. Nor do they light a lamp and put it under a basket, but on a lampstand, and it gives light to all who are in the house. Let your light so shine before men, that they may see your good works and glorify your Father in heaven."

When Glenda and I used to lead short-term mission trips, church board after church board told us that their congregation members were not prepared for missions work—oh, maybe a construction project, but not REAL mission work, not real service and evangelism... In so doing, they effectively cover the lamp of the individuals in the congregation with a basket. They then proceed to keep the congregation members so ridiculously busy doing "churchy" things every day of the week that they have hidden their city on a hill. Like the agents and the publishing houses hoping to draw attention to themselves with quick hits, too many churches today say they are equipping the saints, and then discourage them from going out into the world. This is just a kind of spiritual masturbation, as believers only interact with other believers, and nothing of consequence to change the world takes place.

For the light of the world to mean anything, it has to be IN THE WORLD! The world does not need more Christian school school teachers: it needs more GOOD school teachers, who happen to be Christian, and love their students with a sacrificial love that shows the students their worth. The world does not need more Christian music musicians: it needs more GOOD musicians who happen to be Christian, and who can then impact culture in a relevant and meaningful way. The world does not need more Christian college college professors: it needs more GOOD professors who happen to be believers and dare to teach the truth, even if it does not fit the prevalent metanarrative.

And so on.

Here's the truth: YOU are the light of the world. And YOU shine in your own way that no one else can, so do NOT let somebody try to hide your light.

No, leave the cloisters, get on out into that world, and SHINE! Let people read your life like the amazing book it is!

You've got something to say, and the world needs to hear it!

January 23

I watch as Glenda prepares for her upcoming art show, and she is always asking the question "When will I be as good as I want to be?" If she is like most humans who have a sense of drive, and purpose, the answer is never, as those with the greatest of gifts are always pushing to better themselves.

This was true with the Apostle Paul. Talk about a type "A" personality! Hey, the guy didn't even have a moped, but he made the journey from the Middle East To Europe and back time and time again.

But he still didn't feel like he had it. He recognized he needed more.

Philippians 3:10-14

"I want to know Christ—yes, to know the power of his resurrection and participation in his sufferings, becoming like him in his death, and so, somehow, attaining to the resurrection from the dead. Not that I have already obtained all this, or have already arrived at my goal, but I press on to take hold of that for which Christ Jesus took hold of me. Brothers and sisters, I do not consider myself yet to have taken hold of it. But one thing I do: Forgetting what is behind and straining toward what is ahead, I press on toward the goal to win the prize for which God has called me heavenward in Christ Jesus."

When I read that, I hear Paul's passion, his desire, leaping from the page. Damascus road experience and all, he's "Hey I'm not there, not where I want to even be..." But he presses on, knowing that the goal lay ahead.

And it is not even by our own power that we can attain that goal, for God gives us His strength, as we see in the previous chapter, where Paul had written "for it is God who works in you both to will and to do for His good pleasure." It is God who works in us, His strength, His will, to bring us to the point of dreaming the dreams He has already dreamt for us.

But oh how we sound like six-year-olds in the back of the car yelling "Are we there yet!?!?!?" Priceless! Haha!

No, no we are not, but we are on the road, and we do know who is driving...

January 24

Peace. I find it very depressing that the Oxford English Dictionary defines it as "freedom from, or a cessation of, war or hostilities; the state of a nation or community in which it is not at war with another." The OED defines peace in a negative—that is, what it is not: not war, not violence, not hostility.

But isn't there a drawing in our hearts that lets us know that peace should be so much more?

John 14:27

"Peace I leave with you, My peace I give to you; not as the world gives do I give to you. Let not your heart be troubled, neither let it be afraid."

When Christ said these words, he knew His crucifixion was imminent, and yet, He is putting the feelings and needs of those around Him first, promising to leave them with peace. But this is a peace that is not as the world gives, not just a cessation of hostilities, though that is a portion of the meaning, the Greek word here for "peace" is "eirene," which has a literal meaning of "a harmonious relationship." It carries with it a sense of reconciliation, specifically reconciliation and harmony between God and man.

So we have Christ, at a time in His life when He is anticipating His own torturous death, promising to leave His followers with a harmonious relationship between them and God. A reconciliation born out of love, paid for in sacrifice.

The peace of God is never imposed by force, but instead given in love.

The world is not a peaceful place. Anyone saying anything else is trying to sell you something. But think on this: in Christ, we have been reconciled to, and have a harmonious relationship with, God. And that, my friends, transcends a mere cessation of violence or hostilities. It is the root of a love relationship with God. If you internalize that view of the world, your perspective will change.

And if God is for you, in the ultimate sense, how can one remain troubled? How can one remain afraid?

I wish you peace as you go forward...

January 25

Faith. Hope. Two wonderful characteristics, two wonderful gifts. Both faith and hope take us from the present to the future. That is, they look forward, to how things might be, how things will be, and past the reality of today. Interestingly, there will come a time when faith and hope will cease to exist. This cessation will occur because when we are fully in the presence of God, we will exist totally in the moment. As C.S. Lewis noted, "The horizon ceases to be the horizon when you get there."

So true.

When we will be with God in totality, there will be no need to look past the moment, no need to trust that some future good will come, for we will be there. Love, however, now that is eternal! The need for faith will be replaced with knowledge. The need for hope will be replaced with present reality in God's presence. Love, that will never change!

1st Corinthians 13:8-13

"Love never fails. But where there are prophecies, they will cease; where there are tongues, they will be stilled; where there is knowledge, it will pass away. For we know in part and we prophesy in part, but when perfection comes, the imperfect disappears. When I was a child, I talked like a child, I thought like a child, I reasoned like a child. When I became a man, I put childish ways behind me. Now we see but a poor reflection as in a mirror; then we shall see face to face. Now I know in part; then I shall know fully, even as I am fully known. And now these three remain: faith, hope and love. But the greatest of these is love."

Faith and Hope—are needed for a time that is not yet mature, yet they shall eventually be put away.

Love.

That is living the stuff of heaven right now.

J anuary 26

   As I've reconnected with folks from my past, I have been amazed at how many of them have grown as humans. They've become more loving, increasingly generous, progressing in their work to help others, basically, more real. Then some have not grown a bit, maybe even digressed.

I enjoy spending time with those who are real.

Becoming real is a process, a progression of love. That, however, does not mean it is painless. Consider the words of Margery Williams, from The Velveteen Rabbit: "'It doesn't happen all at once,' said the Skin Horse. 'You become. It takes a long time. That's why it doesn't happen often to people who break easily, or have sharp edges, or who have to be carefully kept. Generally, by the time you are Real, most of your hair has been loved off, and your eyes drop out and you get loose in the joints and very shabby. But these things don't matter at all, because once you are Real you can't be ugly, except to people who don't understand.'" Becoming real is a process of love, but it frankly does not happen to everyone.

Here's how Paul put it:

Romans 5:1-5

"Therefore, having been justified by faith, we have peace with God through our Lord Jesus Christ, through whom also we have access by faith into this grace in which we stand, and rejoice in hope of the glory of God. And not only that, but we also glory in tribulations, knowing that tribulation produces perseverance; and perseverance, character; and character, hope. Now hope does not disappoint, because the love of God has been poured out in our hearts by the Holy Spirit who was given to us."

No, the process of becoming real takes time and involves tribulations. Like the fur getting rubbed off of a child's stuffed animal, as the child cries him/herself to sleep while hugging the plush, as God uses us, we face hardship, showing, working out, and sharing the love of God with others. But in that process, yes, we become worn, but also, we develop perseverance, character, and hope.

And we make a difference. And we become real.

Again, as the skin horse said to the Velveteen Rabbit, "'The Boy's Uncle made me Real," he said. "That was a great many years ago; but once you are Real you can't become unreal again. It lasts for always.'"

These are hard times, but I have watched so many of you who don't have sharp edges, or break easily, or need to be carefully kept, reach out to help others, often at great expense to yourself, bearing many tribulations in the process. And your perseverance has grown, as has your character and your hope. You may feel well worn, shabby even, but you are loved, real.

And you have made a difference, changing the world one life at a time. You've become real.

And "you can't become unreal again. It lasts for always."

As do you, in Christ.

January 27

I love to cook, and am fascinated with culinary history. In the USA, one thing stands out in the last century: in the 1950s and 60s, the culinary culture shifted to speed and convenience, instead of quality and taste. 1 lb ground beef, a can of this, a packet of dried whatever, some frozen that, and voila, a casserole! Except it wasn't a true casserole, nor was it healthy or tasty. And with the convenience of highly processed foods came a rise in cancer, type II diabetes, and obesity, as our society became bloated.

About fifteen years ago I learned something that revolutionized my cooking: time is my friend. Now, when I make fried chicken, I get a dry rub on the bird a full 36 hours before it is time to dredge and fry. Short ribs? They braise for 10-12 hours. Smoking a brisket? Dry rub for 24 hours before starting the smoker, and then smoke for at least eighteen hours.

Time allows the spices to do their work, bringing about a richness in perception, in flavor, in pleasure, that convenience just can't match.

There is a similar corollary with our souls and with our minds.

Philippians 4:8-9

"Finally, brothers and sisters, whatever is true, whatever is honorable, whatever is right, whatever is pure, whatever is lovely, whatever is commendable, if there is any excellence and if anything worthy of praise, think about these things. As for the things you have learned and received and heard and seen in me, practice these things, and the God of peace will be with you."

Today we live in a society of highly processed, convenient "spirituality," and many of us have become nothing more than bloated believers.

Our thoughts are the spices of our emotional and spiritual lives. We live in a society that rewards aggression over contemplativeness and pushes productivity over depth and quality. But we don't have to buy it. The mind that is absorbed by instant gratification, convenience, highly processed sound bite theology, the push to climb that ladder, well that mind will ensure that the emotions of that person will never know peace, for their souls are either marinating in crap or convenience.

William Henry once noted "To live content with small means, to seek elegance rather than luxury, and refinement rather than fashion; to be worthy, not respectable, and wealthy, not rich; to study hard, think quietly, talk gently, act frankly; to listen to stars and birds, to babes and sages, with open heart; to bear all cheerfully, do all bravely, await events, hurry never. In a word, to let the spiritual, unbidden and unconscious, grow up through the common. This is to be my symphony" Oh the simplicity of elegance, the purity of refinement...

True spirituality does not grow through chaos or disruption; but instead through a steadfast focus on what is true, honorable, right, pure, lovely, and commendable. And note the tactile nature of each of those things. They are not flights of fancy or the thrill of cheap entertainment.

True spirituality is the antithesis of the bloated believer.

Convenience has no depth of flavor, and we live in the current of convenience, but here's the deal: every piece of trash, every dead fish flows with the current. Only that which is truly alive can swim upstream.

January 28

There can never be a conference on "radical relevance." That is because the two words are contradictory. Cultural relevance means that not just one person, but a slew of people have gotten to an idea or way of thinking first. It is the defining point of current thinking and contemporary culture. It has no new ideas of its own. And yet a broad swath of the Church in the US strives to be "relevant," oftentimes spending small fortunes on church growth consultants on how to increase their relevancy.

And yet scripture calls neither the Church nor Christians as individuals to be "relevant."

The word is not even used in the Bible. Old or New Testament. Not once.

No, we are called to so much more:

Mathew 5:43-45

"You have heard that it was said, 'You shall love your neighbor and hate your enemy.' But I say to you, love your enemies and pray for those who persecute you, so that you may prove yourselves to be sons of your Father who is in heaven; for He causes His sun to rise on the evil and the good, and sends rain on the righteous and the unrighteous."

Matthew 6:24

"No one can serve two masters. Either you will hate the one and love the other, or you will be devoted to the one and despise the other. You cannot serve both God and money."

Luke 9:23-25

"Then He said to them all, "If anyone desires to come after Me, let him deny himself, and take up his cross daily, and follow Me. For whoever desires to save his life will lose it, but whoever loses his life for My sake will save it. For what profit is it to a man if he gains the whole world, and is himself destroyed or lost?"

Matthew 25:41-45

"Then He will also say to those on the left hand, 'Depart from Me, you cursed, into the everlasting fire prepared for the devil and his angels: for I was hungry and you gave Me no food; I was thirsty and you gave Me no drink; I was a stranger and you did not take Me in, naked and you did not clothe Me, sick and in prison and you did not visit Me.' "Then they also will answer Him, saying, 'Lord, when did we see You hungry or thirsty or a stranger or naked or sick or in prison, and did not minister to You?' Then He will answer them, saying, 'Assuredly, I say to you, inasmuch as you did not do it to one of the least of these, you did not do it to Me.'"

Actively loving one's enemies, Making the binary choice between God and money, Utter self-sacrifice, ministering to those in need, no matter how icky or inconvenient, and the list goes on and on and on. These are not culturally relevant actions, but instead a radical transformative lifestyle, and that is what we are called to. As G.K. Chesterton wrote, "The

Christian ideal has not been tried and found wanting. It has been found difficult; and left untried." Truth. Even in most "churches."

As of this writing in the US this past year, there are more people that, for the first time in American history, reject houses of worship instead of choosing to attend them. Why? Frankly, I hypothesize that the institutional church has succeeded in becoming relevant, and as such, has nothing to offer, as it flows along with the current of the day. It is the protector of old mores, the voice of the idealization of the values of a mythical shire long since departed. It looks back, not forward. It is relevant.

It is a great many things, but one thing it is not: Radical.

And we are called to radical love, radical forgiveness, radical giving, radical sacrifice, and radical service. We are called to these actions, and to communicate with our society in a loving, accepting way. We are called to radical inclusion, but not to relevance.

Have a great day, and for God's sake, literally, don't be relevant...

January 29

When colonization reached the western portion of the United States, there was little to no manufacturing. The towns depended heavily on traders to bring manufactured goods such as pots, pans, tools, and the like. Villagers depended on the arrival of the traders to keep the basics of life going. As such, when they heard the sound of a loud supply wagon approaching, their spirits fell, because a fully loaded wagon makes little noise. It was always the empty or nearly empty wagon that made the most noise, calling attention to itself.

Plato noted something similar – "An empty vessel makes the loudest sound..." But Plato was talking about people, ending the sentence with "so they who have the least wit are the greatest babblers."

The braggart is always the one devoid of real accomplishment, and confidence is silent, while insecurities are loud. Yet a great many seek fame and fortune, while the pursuit of these things is void and empty, antithetical to the pursuit of true spirituality and the knowledge of God. Oh, those things may come of their own, yet they are not to be the focus of our pursuits.

Psalm 27:1-2

"Do not boast about tomorrow, For you do not know what a day may bring.

Let another praise you, and not your own mouth; A stranger, and not your own lips."

Thursday we spent the afternoon with a lady who has done amazing things in our community to aid in the rescue of the street dogs here in Mexico. She never once mentioned or pointed to herself, but instead to the work that needed to be done. My good friend Mithi Mukherjee just won one of the University of Colorado's top honors. She has remained silent about it, even though she is easily the top scholar in the world regarding Indian jurisprudence. Still, other friends work to support a local orphanage and teach ESL to the children of the neighboring village. They will point to the work, but never to themselves.

And then there are those, like certain notable politicians, whose ignorance demands that they talk about and point to themselves, because they have no other knowledge or accomplishments to bring attention to.

There is a quiet confidence in real accomplishment, but yes, it is true that the emptier the wagon, the more noise it makes.

Fame, fortune. These are fleeting at best and only of value if they are given away.

But seek first the Kingdom of God...

Do that, and you will be filled with the Love of God, and that needs to be acted on, instead of just clanging about.

Some food for thought as we prioritize our upcoming day!

January 30

I love gardening, and am very excited that, having planted fourteen Zinnia seeds, and ten Lupine seeds, that all of them have sprouted, and are now growing! Of course, this is Mexico, and everything will grow here. I'm convinced that if one of my toenail clippings fell on the soil, the next week there would be a small toe growing from the ground!

The day each of the seedlings broke through the ground, they started to bend toward the direction of the sunlight. This is through a process called phototropism, and the plants are hard-wired to do this. Why? Because the sunlight is what provides the plant with the energy it needs to grow, to thrive, so the plant reaches towards the beneficial light with all it has.

The process of reaching toward the light helps the plant to grow, but what about the night? Will plants grow in the dark? The answer is yes! Plants absorb energy from the sun through photosynthesis during the day and grow during the day. But in reaching for the proper nutrition found in the light, they absorb more energy than they can use during the day, so at night, with the surplus energy, they stretch out, even more, growing at a faster rate, as they search for light!

1 Peter 2:2-3

"Like newborn babies, crave pure spiritual milk, so that by it you may grow up in your salvation, now that you have tasted that the Lord is good."

The plant is hard-wired to reach for the proper nutrition it needs, We, however, have a free will, and so it is our choice as to what we reach to for our nourishment. And frankly, it is too often easy to reach for the wrong thing. As spiritual beings living in a material world, that which is tactile like attention, recognition, material prosperity, and the like provide false equivalencies to the intangibles that are of greatest importance.

Hummingbirds crave sweetness, but attempt to sate that desire with Splenda, which is a thousand times sweeter than sugar, and the hummingbird will die because there is no nutrition to be had.

Same with us.

We can seek to quench our inherent spiritual hunger with a host of things that have no value, or we can choose to taste and see that the Lord is good.

Many of us have been going through dark times of late, but like the plants mentioned above, if we have chosen to nourish our souls with the presence of God, we will find that that surplus of nutrition will turn the dark time into one of the periods of greatest growth for us.

Christ described Himself in part as "the Light of the world," Let us then choose to bend in His direction. As Victor Hugo noted, "The pupil dilates in darkness and in the end finds light, just as the soul dilates in misfortune and in the end finds God."

There is no darkness that light cannot pierce. Let us then choose to bend towards Christ, the light of the world.

January 31

Isn't love grand? That excitement before a date, the tingle of electricity as your hands accidentally brush, the stirring of emotion, of passion, of a renewed sense of the intensity of life itself. Romantic love is in and of itself its own reward, which, if we are lucky, transforms us into a better person.

Then there is love the discipline: the parent caring for their special needs child, the husband or wife caring for their spouse with dementia, the child caring for their terminally ill parent, the man or woman touching the hand of the beggar as they give them cash, because they know that the human touch is more healing than the mere money...

Romantic love, if we are lucky, may change us for the better. The discipline of love always makes this world a nobler place.

When the Pharisees asked Christ what the greatest commandment was, this is how He replied:

Matthew 22:37-40

"'You shall love the Lord your God with all your heart, with all your soul, and with all your mind.' This is the first and great commandment. And the second is like it: 'You shall love your neighbor as yourself.' On these two commandments hang all the Law and the Prophets."

The word Christ used here was "Agapao," a verb, which means the act of selfless love. There is inherent in the meaning a sense of sacrifice, a call to that which is not easy. It is at the very least giving of ourselves and acting out of love to the unlovable, for if we are not loving the unlovable, then what virtue have we expressed?

G.K. Chesterton once noted, "The Bible tells us to love our neighbors, and also to love our enemies; probably because they are generally the same people." All humor aside, oft times he is correct.

We love ourselves by working for our greatest benefit. No matter our missteps, and we know we have them, we still work to feed ourselves, house ourselves, and clothe ourselves. The gut-wrenching question then is, do we also, with as much passion and zeal, work for the benefit of our neighbor, our fellow man, regardless of his or her missteps, as we may perceive them? If not, if we are waiting for them to be loveable enough, good enough, then we have turned the wisdom of Christ into a mere platitude.

The love Christ is talking about is a verb, an action, a service, a sacrifice, not simply a state of being, as in "being in love." And it has no preconditions as to merit.

You made it through the month!

Let's get busy!

Chapter Two

February

February 1

There have been times in my life when my heart utterly broke. Most recently, it was the passing of Rogue the Dogue. Before that, the death of Millie the Wonderdog. I've cried plenty of times, but those times, and a few others, I wept. Tears flowed down my face in uncontrollable sobs of anguish. My tear ducts had the dry heaves, and my body shook. The Oxford English Dictionary defines weeping as "Manifest pain, misery, and grief by tears accompanied by sobs and inarticulate moans." Yeah, partially correct, and the back spasms, and soul ripping agony...

The Gospel of John tells the story of Lazarus, one of Jesus' best friends. Lazarus became ill, and his sisters, Martha and Mary sent for Jesus, asking him to come and heal him. Two days later, Jesus went and Lazarus was already dead. Jesus saw Mary and Martha weeping, along with the rest of Lazarus' family and friends. Scripture records His response in the shortest, but one of the most telling verses in scripture.

John 11:35

"Jesus Wept."

Jesus went on to raise Lazarus from the dead—that had been his plan all along, but the grief of those around Him so moved Him to compassion and empathy that He wept—not shed a tear, as so many movies portray, but wept. The tears of soul-wrenching grief.

And He knew that He was going to raise Lazarus from the dead, but out of His love for, and understanding of the pain of those around him, He wept. Sobbed.

Then He went about bringing His perfect solution.

Friends, I know some of you have been deeply hurt of late, that you have wept. And let me tell you this—God knows. He holds the solution to your travail, but in seeing your pain, He weeps with you. He feels not just for you, but alongside you. The heart of God flows in your tears, as He feels with you.

And He never tells you to "suck it up," or to "just get on with things."

It is easy to think of God as distant but when you cry, He shares the depth of your pain, and then brings healing.

But healing is always on the other side of pain, like resurrection is on the other side of death.

One who has healed, though, is a different person. Deeper, more compassionate, more appreciative of life.

But if you are weeping today, know these three things:

Jesus is weeping with you.

Resurrection is coming.

And one day God will wipe away every tear.

Remember that God stands by you during the hardest of times, not just feeling for, but feeling with you.

February 2

A good friend told me a week or so ago that the big thing that turned him away from the church was his curiosity. He'd ask reasonable questions, only to be told, "You shouldn't be asking that."

What a pile of excrement.

Consider this:

Matthew 18:1-5

"At that time the disciples came to Jesus and asked, "Who, then, is the greatest in the kingdom of heaven?" He called a little child to him, and placed the child among them. And he said: "Truly I tell you, unless you change and become like little children, you will never enter the kingdom of heaven. Therefore, whoever takes the lowly position of this child is the greatest in the kingdom of heaven. And whoever welcomes one such child in my name welcomes me."

The faith of a child is defined by two things: a sense of wonder, and unbridled curiosity. It is not "innocent"—I've known too many children to believe that! It is not simplistic—again, back to that unbridled curiosity.

Linguistically, a child's best friend is the interrogative. "Why?" "How?" "What if?"

With each question, the child seeks to go deeper, to understand more, to know.

Until that is punished out of them, along with their creativity, usually at a very young age.

Moreover, with a few notable exceptions, the church is very good at doing that to its believers as well.

Like many, I came to know Christ in high school and had a host of questions. Youth pastors were of absolutely no help, in that they wanted to make me into an ideal Presbyterian, Baptist, or Methodist, with a relationship with Christ as secondary to their denominational prejudices. Fortunately, I met a great YoungLife leader, who encouraged, and even challenged my intellectual pursuit.

My point is this—Ask the questions. Pursue the knowledge. Demand the intellectual integrity you deserve from the clergy, and lovingly do not tolerate cheap and easy, intellectually lazy answers, like "God said it, I believe it, and that settles it."

Never, ever, let anyone punish your spiritual curiosity out of you. Reach out to touch the mind of God, in wonder and inquisitiveness.

February 3

It's been said that 99% of humanity will expend 99% of their effort to stay within their comfort zone. As a historian and one who studies the human condition, I'd have to agree with that, except for the 1% who are truly self-actualized, those who live in constant amazement. Here's the deal: my wife Glenda and I have learned that everything of real value we have ever received has been on the other side of fear. Oh desire can excite, but it is a cheap counterfeit of the real thing—again, everything of real value we have ever received has been on the other side of fear.

Inaction builds cowardice, but as Eleanor Roosevelt noted, "You gain strength, courage, and confidence by every experience in which you really stop to look fear in the face. You are able to say to yourself, 'I have lived through this horror. I can take the next thing that comes along.' You must do the thing you think you cannot do." Truth. Courage is a muscle that increases in strength when one exercises it.

Jesus has sent the disciples across the Sea of Galilee in a boat at night, as He withdraws to pray. Then along comes a storm...

Matthew 14:24-31

"But the boat was already a long distance from the land, battered by the waves; for the wind was contrary. And in the fourth watch of the night He came to them, walking on the sea. When the disciples saw Him walking on the sea, they were terrified, and said, "It is a ghost!" And they cried out in fear. But immediately Jesus spoke to them, saying, "Take courage, it is I; do not be afraid."

Peter responded and said to Him, "Lord, if it is You, command me to come to You on the water." And He said, "Come!" And Peter got out of the boat and walked on the water, and came toward Jesus. But seeing the wind, he became frightened, and when he began to sink, he cried out, saying, "Lord, save me!" Immediately Jesus reached out with His hand and took hold of him, and said to him, "You of little faith, why did you doubt?"

I've seen the legalists rip all heart from this passage too many times. Jesus tells them don't be afraid, I'm not a ghost! And Peter's response is awesome "Then Lord, command me to come to you!" And the word that Peter uses here for "command" is the strongest Greek word possible to convey that meaning. It means a command in the form of an imperative demand. And Jesus does so. In my mind's eye, I see Him laughing as he does. In Peter's request of Christ, basically, "Lord, if it is You, demand that I come to you," Peter steps to the other side of fear. Balls of steel, Peter. And he walks on water. Oh, he stumbles, he sinks, But Christ, and again in my mind's eye I see him laughing as he does this, reaches out his hand, lifting Peter up, and lovingly, jokingly teases him about his faith.

A different, though linguistically and grammatically accurate portrayal than you hear most Sunday's eh?

It is easy for us to say we want to serve God, to be working with Him where He is working, but, hey, we're in a boat, and there's a storm… And I know boats, I'm comfortable in a boat…

But Jesus is outside of our comfort zone, in the storm.

Here is my challenge to you, Join me in this short prayer—And I'd be lying if I didn't admit that my hands are shaking as I type this… "Jesus, I want to see You and be with You where you are, where You are working. Command me to come to you. Amen"

My friends, much love to you all. I hope to see you on the other side of fear.

February 4

Epictetus, one of my favorite philosophers, wisely wrote "First learn the meaning of what you would say, then speak." Wise words, oh so often ignored!

When we moved to Mexico, our dogs were on a different flight. They ended up in Mexico City, where they remained in their crates for three days before finally being placed on a plane to Guadalajara. We hired a man named Arturo to drive us to the airport to pick up the dogs. He quoted 1,000 pesos for the job—Very reasonable considering the trip, the size of our dogs, etc. On the way to the airport, an accident on the freeway caused us an hour delay. Arturo had another job and was going to miss it. He called to arrange for someone to take care of it for him, but he missed out on the pay. When we got to the airport, our dogs, covered in feces and urine, as no one had let them out of their crates for days, strained to get out to us. As we waited on the tarmac, it started to rain. We opened the dog crates one by one, and each time, though the pups were filthy, Arturo got down on his knees, hugged the dogs, and carried them to his van. On the way back, another wreck on the freeway caused a delay, so again Arturo had to arrange for another driver to pick up his fare. When we got home, I said, "Hey, this was a bigger job than the one you quoted, how much do I owe you. Arturo said, "I stand by my quote, not a peso more."

Arturo and I became friends, and I have done business with him and his family ever since. He is a man of his word.

Matthew 5:33-37

"Again you have heard that it was said to those of old, 'You shall not swear falsely, but shall perform your oaths to the Lord.' But I say to you, do not swear at all: neither by heaven, for it is God's throne; nor by the earth, for it is His footstool; nor by Jerusalem, for it is the city of the great King. Nor shall you swear by your head, because you cannot make one hair white or black. But let your 'Yes' be 'Yes,' and your 'No,' 'No.' For whatever is more than these is from the evil one."

Let your 'Yes' be 'Yes,' and your 'No,' 'No. Why is that so hard for some people? Know the meaning of the words, say them, and then follow through. That is the basis of integrity, and integrity is simply doing what is right instead of what is fun or convenient. 25 years ago, Robert Fulghum wrote the book *All I Really Need to Know I Learned in Kindergarten*. One of the things we need to know that we all were taught, but only some learned in kindergarten is that if you say you're going to do something, do it. It is a trustworthy statement that the person who has to make promises to be believed is a person who is also adept at making excuses.

Some people bring results, others bring rationalizations. Which one do you want to do business with? Which one do you want to be? Your reputation is built on the results of your choices, and when your yes is yes, and your no is no, you have nothing to fear, because you have nothing to hide. When we give people our word, let us always remember that Christ defines Himself, in part as "the Word."

Have a great day!

February 5

Sassy the Superpup is our Golden Retriever. She is sweet, beautiful, and very athletic. I've seen her clear a five-foot fence without effort several times, much to my chagrin. She can negotiate any kind of terrain with fierce determination. Except at bedtime...

At night, and only at night, when Sassy knows we're going to bed, she will put her front paws on the bed, and wait until I give her a butt hoist up onto the mattress. Oh, she'll get down in the middle of the night for sure, but then she'll want back up. She will put her front paws up on the bed, and then gently poke my shoulder with her nose. I will then get out of bed, and hoist her butt back up on the bed again, though she could easily jump over the entire length of the bed without a thought.

When it's bedtime though, cuddle time, she wants that extra bit of help, the reminder that she is wanted, and also an expression that she is not taking her spot on the bed with us for granted.

And she always gives me a gentle kiss of appreciation for each lift.

Psalm 46:1-3

"God is our refuge and strength, an ever-present help in trouble. Therefore we will not fear, though the earth give way and the mountains fall into the heart of the sea, though its waters roar and foam and the mountains quake with their surging."

And:

Romans 8:14-16

"For those who are led by the Spirit of God are the children of God. The Spirit you received does not make you slaves, so that you live in fear again; rather, the Spirit you received brought about your adoption to sonship. And by him we cry, "Abba, Father."

Yes, God is always there for us in times of trouble, but there is more—He desires the intimacy with us, literally the cuddle time. The word "Abba" is Aramaic, meaning literally "Daddy." "Daddy God" is how He wants us to know Him. And with the concept of "Daddy," that intimacy of expression is the very idea of one who WANTS to take us in His arms, WANTS us to sit on his lap, WANTS to be known in a comforting, safe fashion.

Friends, at the time of this writing we are still in a pandemic, something none of us has ever seen before. And yes, God is there for us in times of trouble, but there is so much more, He wants intimacy, He wants us to come not just in the times of trouble, but with the innocent questions, with the joys, when we want a butt hoist up to know that it's OK to cuddle, that being with Him is a safe space.

I hope this gives you a smile to start your day, a confidence to turn to God with the big things, yes, but also with the little joys, the questions, and the need for assurance.

Because He is Daddy God...

February 6

Ahh, Spa day!! Relaxation, hot springs, a massage... The definition of comfort. And spa days are needed from time to time. Those rewards for a job well done, a reminder that it is not just OK, but needed from time to time for us to relax. Yeah, Spa time is great.

Just not every day...

Here's the deal, one cannot be committed to one's dream and one's comfort zone as well.

Very little productivity takes place in the spa.

Spas are wonderful, peaceful, safe harbors, and a boat is always safest in a harbor. But spending its' life in a harbor is not what a sailing craft was designed to do.

Consider this:

Galatians 2:20

"I have been crucified with Christ; it is no longer I who live, but Christ lives in me; and the life which I now live in the flesh I live by faith in the Son of God, who loved me and gave Himself for me."

In Seminary we learned how to dance all around this verse, without actually getting to the meat—"I have been crucified with Christ..." We were taught (put on a deep, sanctifying tone here) "This refers to where we are positionally in Christ..." Well, in part, BUT, if you are ever serious about ministry, or service, guess what—You are going to get your butt kicked. You will be crucified at some time or many times by those you are trying to serve.

Logically, then that is to be avoided...but it goes on to say that we are to live by faith.

Not common sense.

Not by worldly wisdom.

By faith.

It is only when we are living by faith that the sailing vessel of our lives leaves the harbor. We leave the comfort, the safety, and enter into a journey of discovery, of wonder, of potentiality that we could never have dreamed of had we stayed in port.

No, one cannot be committed to one's dreams and one's comfort zone.

Leaving harbor is frightening, and there will be wounds, no doubt about it. But living in faith is letting the power of Christ fill your life, like the wind into the sails of a boat.

And where that will carry a person, one will only know if they only choose to leave the spa or harbor.

February 7

Chaucer, our English Setter, is a large dog—About 55-60 pounds. But at night, he becomes a puppy again, insisting to curl up with his head in the crook of my neck as we sleep. But last night...

The dreaded nose whistle.

Yes, a shrill whistle emanated from my nose every time I exhaled. Chaucer's head bolted up! He gently nudged my nose with his. I exhaled again. This time he more forcefully bumped my nose with his. Another exhale, another whistle. Chaucer then pulled out his front left paw and whacked it across my nose. Tears streamed from my eyes, and I let out an unflattering pejorative.

But the whistle stopped.

And Chaucer tucked his head under my chin and fell instantly back to sleep.

Yes, some noises can be very annoying...

1 Corinthians 13:1-3

"If I speak with the tongues of mankind and of angels, but do not have love, I have become a noisy gong or a clanging cymbal. If I have the gift of prophecy and know all mysteries and all knowledge, and if I have all faith so as to remove mountains, but do not have love, I am nothing. And if I give away all my possessions to charity, and if I surrender my body so that I may glory, but do not have love, it does me no good."

A noisy gong or a clanging cymbal...I'd probably add an accordion into the mix, maybe bagpipes, and apparently my nose whistle, but that's just me. The thing is this, an action done without love is not just an exercise in futility, it is annoying. To put it into culinary terms, one can make a nutritious meal, but if it has no flavor (like a lot of the stuff from many a Church pot luck...), it brings no joy at all.

All too often, Love is the undiscovered or unused ingredient as we live our lives. And yes, we do leave a taste in our wake. Is there any good flavor at all?

Paul lists five spiritual gifts here—Gifts of great power and significance. Gifts that when used are highly visible. Yet, if they are exercised without love, not only has nothing of real value been accomplished, but we've also managed to annoy those around us, reflecting poorly on God, the gift giver in the first place.

Too often, we are like the dog, running from pillar to post, leaving nothing but a wet spot at each stop.

Love, though, requires us to slow down, be contemplative, take the time to feel, and then, and only then, to act. Doing so makes beautiful music to the ears and brings true flavor to life, a heady, pleasant aroma to all around us.

And it brings pleasure to God.

February 8

Ahhh, the zero-sum game. Frankly, I can't think of too many things that have culturally and spiritually damaged United States society more. Oh, don't get me wrong! I love a game of softball or racquetball, and I used to be involved in competitive cycling. But the internalization of the idea of the Zero-Sum Mentality—The "I won, which means YOU lost," "I'm a winner, which means YOU'RE A loser," has established false divides and hostilities. The thinking sets up a demonization of one's opponent, a belittling, when in fact, the members of the opposing team have the same desire to perform well, the same hopes, and the same fears. The internalization of the Zero-Sum Mentality negates the free exchange of ideas, as one who disagrees with our point of view must, then, be wrong.

In high school, before a game of football or basketball with another school, the coaches still had a teammate lead the team in prayer. That prayer was always for victory, which sickened me even then, for that meant the humiliation of the other team. Except for one coach, Coach Coleman. I was one of his trainers for varsity basketball. He would have the player who led the prayer pray that the team play to their best ability, play safely, and play with honor. Now that made sense to me because it removed the sense of identity of "winner versus loser" from the equation.

Within the Church, denominationalism, especially, has fostered the internalization of the Zero-Sum mentality. "God loves ME more because I'm a good Baptist, or Presbyterian..." fill in the blank. But the Zero-Sum Mentality is utterly antithetical to Christianity.

Consider this: the phrase "one another" is used one hundred times in the New Testament alone. Here's a smattering:

"...Be at peace with each other." (Mark 9:50).

"...Wash one another's feet." (John 13:14).

"...Love one another..." (John 13:34).

"Be devoted to one another in brotherly love…" (Romans 12:10).

"…Honor one another above yourselves. (Romans 12:10).

"Live in harmony with one another…" (Romans 12:16).

"…Stop passing judgment on one another." (Romans 14:13).

"Accept one another, then, just as Christ accepted you…" (Romans 15:7).

"…Instruct one another." (Romans 15:14).

"…Have equal concern for each other." (I Corinthians 12:25).

"…Serve one another in love." (Galatians 5:13).

Not much room for the Zero-Sum Mentality, if we are serious about following Christ, then, is there? The idea of working together, seeing each other in a "One Another" format radically changes one's behavior.

Or it should.

Zero-Sum Mentality divides, while "One Another" thinking builds a sense of community, service, love, and trust.

I don't know about you, but I think we need a little, no, a heck of a lot more of that.

Keep up the good work, and let's work together to love, to serve one another.

February 9

Background noise. It used to be that whenever I got in my car, I had the radio on. I would always splurge on a good sound system for my car. At home, too, when we were there, the TV was always on. Heck, there was a time when we'd leave it on for the dogs. Even into the start of my Ph.D. program, when I'd read, there was always music playing softly as a backdrop.

Then came the time for comprehensive exams. A four-hour oral exam, in which I had to have the outlines of over 480 books memorized. I turned the radio in my car off, as I needed to use every moment to recite different thesis points to myself in my head. The TV was now only on when we were purposefully watching it. And I sought silence, not music, while reading.

And life got better, as did my relationship with Christ.

No more advertising filling my ears, making me think I needed things that in truth I didn't even want. No more pedantic nonsense written to the lowest common denominator of the consuming public.

Consider these words written about the prophet Elijah, which are descriptive, but, in this instance, I believe it is hermeneutically sound to say that they are prescriptive as well:

1 Kings 19:11-13

"The Lord said, "Go out and stand on the mountain in the presence of the Lord, for the Lord is about to pass by. Then a great and powerful wind tore the mountains apart and shattered the rocks before the Lord, but the Lord was not in the wind. After the wind there was an earthquake, but the Lord was not in the earthquake. After the earthquake came a fire, but the Lord was not in the fire. And after the fire came a gentle whisper. When Elijah heard it, he pulled his cloak over his face and went out and stood at the mouth of the cave. Then a voice said to him, "What are you doing here, Elijah?""

Many things try to catch our attention. Loud things, sometimes-cataclysmic events. For Elijah, it was stone-shattering wind, an earthquake, then a fire.

But God was not in any of those things.

God came to him in a still, small voice.

A whisper.

Our culture pushes us to interact with electronic devices constantly. Part of us even hopes these interactions will bring some kind of wisdom, insight, and growth. But the mind-numbing constancy of background noise is just a counterfeit of truth, a means of plugging our ears to the whisper of God.

The fact is, the meditative, contemplative life is impossible when one's ears are too full of trash to hear the voice of God.

Don't get me wrong—Glenda and I have a top-notch sound system. But it is only on at home when we specifically want to listen to certain pieces of music. We have a nice HDTV. It, too, only operates when we have a specific movie or event we desire to watch.

The rest of the time we hear the birds sing, we hear our breath, and sometimes, sometimes we hear a still, small voice.

February 10

I loved studying business law. It was very basic in many ways: Offer + Acceptance = Contract. In other words, if you offer to do something or provide something for a specific cost, and the other person accepts, you have a binding valid contract, whether it is on paper or not. The rest of business law pivots on this one principle.

In many respects, our relationship and interaction with God are very similar. God offers (and typically pays the price as well) we accept, contract. God will follow through.

It is up to us, though, to act on what we receive.

John 10:9-10

"I am the door; if anyone enters through Me, he will be saved, and will go in and out and find pasture. The thief comes only to steal and kill and destroy; I came so that they would have life, and have it abundantly."

God offers life, and life abundantly. The question is, has one or will one accept that offer? If so, contract. Paid. Binding.

Ok, what now?

The word translated as "life" is the Greek word "Zoe." It is the word we get our word "zoology" from. In this sense, though, it means literally, Life in the absolute sense. Life as God has it. And Christ came not to dribble that out, but to give it abundantly—the Greek word "pereissos," which carries the meaning of "abundance specifically to one's advantage." So, very literally, Christ came to give us Life in that absolute sense—the kind God Himself enjoys, abundantly to our best advantage. And if you've accepted that offer, there is a binding contract in effect, not for some time in the future, but RIGHT NOW.

Here's the question—Are you living it?

Say someone came to you and offered you a brand new Ferrari, gratis. You accept the offer. What do you do now? Park the car in your garage never to be seen again, out of fear of the power, the value of the car? (I know someone who has done just that, by the way...). Or do you drive it? Push it? Test the limits?

If we have accepted it, God has given us this gift of life, and life abundantly right now. Are we parking it in the suburbs, surrounded by people who look like, dress like, think like us, speak with no accents, and always wear color-coordinated clothing? Or are we pushing it to the limits, realizing that as we have benefited, so can we then be a benefit to others?

It's your life. What are you going to do with it, because merely making a living is not living life.

Please take the time to ponder. As for me right now, I'm going to go take my car for a spin...

February 11

My wife LOVES orchids, and today was kind of special, in that Louis, the orchid guy (locally famous for supplying great orchids here) stopped by our house, and yes, I bought an orchid, or more accurately, a colony of many orchids from him. They are growing out of a large piece of bark, about half a meter in length. Louis gave two pieces of advice: Mist the orchids once a week to water them, and do NOT remove them from the tree bark, as that specific tree bark is what they need to survive, to thrive.

Funny how different plants require different growing mediums: beans can take poor soil, and infuse it with nitrogen. Corn requires nitrogen-rich soil, and so on. Some plants require high Ph. levels in soil, others low. But though one may be able to get a plant to live in soil that is less than ideal, the plant will not thrive.

Ephesians 3:16-19

"I pray that out of his glorious riches he may strengthen you with power through his Spirit in your inner being, so that Christ may dwell in your hearts through faith. And I pray that you, being rooted and established in love, may have power, together with all the Lord's holy people, to grasp how wide and long and high and deep is the love of Christ, and to know this love that surpasses knowledge—that you may be filled to the measure of all the fullness of God."

A plant will grow well if it is rooted in the proper medium. Established in that medium, the plant then bears fruit. The fruits that Paul lists here are power, a tactile understanding of the full dimensionality of the Love of Christ, and a filling of that to the measure and fullness of God Himself.

Unlike plants though, we can choose the medium in which we grow, and, for me at least oh so often, those roots want to wander! To tiptoe around to test different soils, but when we abide in, are rooted and established in the Love of God, oh how the growth takes place!

February 12

When we were in Cuba doing mission work, the church pastor I was working with, Daniel, took me to see the comptroller of Bauta, the city we were working in. I was a bit nervous, as he was a high government official. I thought I'd break the ice by talking about accounting theory for municipalities, as I have a finance background, and I'm edgy like that. He stopped me after a few sentences and said "I saw your face in my dream last night, though I've never met you. Tell me what you came here to tell me." Ok, no pressure... So I shared the gospel with him.

He listened intently. Then he said, "Can you lead me in prayer?"

"Sure!" I replied, and did. He then called his wife into the room, and he shared with her and led her in prayer. Then he turned to two of his helpers and told them to get two buckets and fill them with water.

"Why?" I asked.

He said, "Because you and Daniel are going to baptize me in my front yard after we gather the neighbors." We did just that.

Afterward, he said to me, "I am one of the top ten Communist officials in this state's government. One cannot be a Christian and serve in the government. Tomorrow I will do the honorable thing, and resign. I wanted to be baptized in my front yard, neighbors watching, because I wanted all of my neighbors to know why, after tomorrow, that I am unemployed, and that I am not ashamed."

True story, and to this day, I stand amazed that neither my heart nor my head exploded.

That was thirty years ago, and I still see that man's face, and that absolute expression of joy shining through his countenance as we doused him with those buckets of water.

Romans 1:16-17

"For I am not ashamed of the gospel of Christ, for it is the power of God to salvation for everyone who believes, for the Jew first and also for the Greek. For in it the righteousness of

God is revealed from faith to faith; as it is written, 'The just shall live by faith.'"

I'll be quite honest—The majority of my friends do not share my faith. And frankly, I'll respond much more favorably to the person handing me a glass of scotch or a shot of tequila than I will to someone trying to hand me a "Christian Voters Guide." I don't ram my faith down anyone's throats, but folks do know where I stand because I am not ashamed, but I am also not a braggart, for my faith is not of me, but that, too, a gift.

My Cuban friend responded to his acceptance of Christ with honor, resigning from his job the next day. Too many respond by immediately imposing obligations, rules and regs, on others.

So as you start this week, I ask you to look in your heart and take a tally of that which you are not ashamed of. Then ask "How, then, shall I live?"

February 13

Some days it is easy to feel overwhelmed. The aggressive drivers with their "you're number one" gestures, the thoughtless co-worker, the anonymity of the city, the careless gossip, the news of the latest mass shooting... It is easy, for me, anyway, ofttimes to feel besieged, to look around and ask, "What damn difference can I make?"

Moreover, if you are like me, please know that you are not alone in these feelings, as some of the greatest minds, greatest artists, have wrestled with that question. Consider these words by Walt Whitman, penned in 1892:

"Oh me! Oh life! of the questions of these recurring,

Of the endless trains of the faithless, of cities fill'd with the foolish,

Of myself forever reproaching myself, (for who more foolish than I, and who more faithless?)

Of eyes that vainly crave the light, of the objects mean, of the struggle ever renew'd,

Of the poor results of all, of the plodding and sordid crowds I see around me,

Of the empty and useless years of the rest, with the rest me intertwined,

The question, O me! so sad, recurring—What good amid these, O me, O life?

Answer.

That you are here—that life exists and identity,

That the powerful play goes on, and you may contribute a verse."

I know I feel utterly inadequate to the challenges we face, as do many others. But perception is NOT reality!

Romans 8:35-37

"Who shall separate us from the love of Christ? Shall tribulation, or distress, or persecution, or famine, or nakedness, or peril, or sword? As it is written: 'For Your sake we are killed all day long; We are accounted as sheep for the slaughter.' Yet in all these things we are more than conquerors through Him who loved us."

Yes, we feel inadequate, despairing, even, but the reality is, as we face the challenges, we are more than conquerors.

Luke, who wrote the gospel by his name, and the book of Acts, was an educated man, and a brilliant writer. He used an interesting literary device in "The Acts of the Apostles," namely, he wrote the story without a conclusion, without an ending.

Why? How is this of significance?

Because, my friend, "the powerful play goes on, and you may contribute a verse."

Your life in Christ is becoming scripture, and, becoming is a process. Yet, as I see the beauty in you, I for one cannot wait to read your verse.

February 14

Daily it seems, challenges arise in our lives that are larger than we are. Many of them are real, and some are imagined. And as we see them, the line from "Game of Thrones" comes to mind—"For the night is long, and full of terrors." The question is when we encounter such challenges, do we rise to meet them, and if so, how?

This is not a new problem for this generation; it has been a reality since time immemorial.

There have always been giants to fight.

David faced one named Goliath, who had been taunting the army of the Israelites for forty days and nights, as all who saw him pointed to his size and ferocity.

1 Samuel 17: 32-51

"Then David said to Saul, "Let no man's heart fail because of him; your servant will go and fight with this Philistine."

And Saul said to David, "You are not able to go against this Philistine to fight with him; for you are a youth, and he a man of war from his youth...."Moreover David said, "The Lord, who delivered me from the paw of the lion and from the paw of the bear, He will deliver me from the hand of this Philistine. And Saul said to David, "Go, and the Lord be with you!"

So Saul clothed David with his armor, and he put a bronze helmet on his head; he also clothed him with a coat of mail. David fastened his sword to his armor and tried to walk, for he had not tested them. And David said to Saul, "I cannot walk with these, for I have not tested them." So David took them off.

Then he took his staff in his hand; and he chose for himself five smooth stones from the brook, and put them in a shepherd's bag, in a pouch which he had, and his sling was in his hand. And he drew near to the Philistine...

Then David said to the Philistine, "You come to me with a sword, with a spear, and with a javelin. But I come to you in the name of the Lord of hosts, the God of the armies of Israel, whom you have defied. This day the Lord will deliver you into my hand, and I will strike you and take your head from you. And this day I will give the carcasses of the camp of the Philistines to the birds of the air and the wild beasts of the earth, that all the earth may know that there is a God in Israel. Then all this assembly shall know that the Lord does not save with sword and spear; for the battle is the Lord's, and He will give you into our hands."

So it was, when the Philistine arose and came and drew near to meet David, that David hurried and ran toward the army to meet the Philistine. Then David put his hand in his bag and took out a stone; and he slung it and struck the Philistine in his forehead, so that the stone sank into his forehead, and he fell on his face to the earth. So David prevailed over the Philistine with a sling and a stone, and struck the Philistine and killed him. But there was no sword in the hand of David. Therefore David ran and stood over the Philistine, took his sword and drew it out of its sheath and killed him, and cut off his head with it. And when the Philistines saw that their champion was dead, they fled."

Not the cutesy children's Sunday School tale, eh? In fact, I do not think this is a story appropriate for young children.

But for us adults, two primary things come to mind as takeaways: first, NEVER fight wearing another man's armor. Internalize this—God has equipped YOU to face the battles you will face. He has equipped others differently, to face their fights.

Second, and most important—The trained soldiers of the Israelite army, and the king of Israel, focused on the challenge, the danger of Goliath. His size, his ferocity, the quality of his armor and armaments.

They compared themselves to the challenge, and none dared to stand before this man who daily insulted their God. David, though, focused on God, acknowledging that the battle belonged to Him, and not to David. He did not claim responsibility for the fight but instead allowed God to use him, and then gave God credit for the victory.

It's a new day. Giants are waiting. What will your strategies be in facing them?

February 15

A good friend made the point yesterday that when someone says, "'After all I've done for you..." they are revealing that what they did was not for you, at all, but for their own need to control you. Their generosity was just a contract with hidden terms of compliance. Spot On!! Those who do so are vile individuals. Of even greater concern, though are those who attempt to make God in their own image, by ascribing to Him that kind of mentality.

I've heard it from pulpits, church lady types, "Moral Majority" wannabees, and all kinds of legalists. "Salvation is by grace through faith alone, but first, get your act together." They try to make it sound like Jesus came to instill a new legal system, a higher morality.

But here's the deal: morality is nothing but the Satanic counterfeit to holiness.

To be Holy means to be "set apart." In context, "Set apart unto God." And in a proper understanding of theology, we must know that it is God who does the work of setting us apart! We cannot boast.

Christ came, in large part, to undo the work of the legalists, the modern-day Pharisees. When they tried to set the bar high, He raised it even higher, to point out that the attainment of "morality" was impossible, thus showing that we humans needed grace—that is, unmerited favor.

Christ brought the love and grace of God to man in a tangible manner.

Without condition.

Within thirty years of Christ's death and resurrection, legalists, and moralists, tried to re-install law on top of grace.

Paul said, translating literally, that he wished they would "castrate themselves."

Christ's message of love and grace was consistent with that of the old testament, when "Abraham believed God, and it was reckoned to him as righteousness.," and this:

Psalm 46:1

"God is our refuge and strength, an ever-present help in trouble."

Notice that there is no conditionality here! No "God is our refuge and strength, an ever-present help in trouble to those who are good enough." No, His help is based solely on our need for it, flowing from His love.

Many ascribe to Jesus an "After all I've done for you..." mentality—When you hear someone trying to play that moralistic one-upmanship, trying to make it sound like Jesus requires certain rules and regs as a condition for His grace, tell them to castrate themselves. You'll be in good company.

I know I've come across as terse, but I am sickened by how many people have been put off of anything to do with God by the legalists, the church-lady types. God's love stands without condition. Anyone who says differently is wasting air.

February 16

I LOVE the thunderstorms here in the mountains of South Central Mexico! They are magnificent! And, living in the crater of a volcano, the claps of thunder will shake our four-hundred-year-old house. Before living here, I was impressed by the thunderstorms that would roll through Atlanta. Big raindrops, bright flashes of lightning... And Millie the Wonderdog.

Oh, how I miss Millie the Wonderdog! She had a larger-than-life personality and was the definition of loyalty. Millie would challenge every thunderstorm. At the first peal of thunder, Millie would BOLT out of the doggy door, run downstairs, and sit in the EXACT CENTER of the backyard. At every crack of thunder, she would loudly howl a challenge. After the storm passed, which sometimes took hours, she would come in, cold, wet, and tired.

And she could have let herself in the whole time.

John 16:33

"These things I have spoken to you so that in Me you may have peace. In the world you have tribulation, but take courage; I have overcome the world."

Millie the Wonderdog had her choice—stay inside, in the peace of the house, or go out into the storm.

As those who trust in Christ, we have the same choice as to where we abide. Simply put, when we are abiding in Christ, we have peace.

Oh, that is not to say that there isn't challenging work to be done, but one can accomplish much while at peace!

And yet some consistently choose to run out into each storm, exhausting themselves by barking at the thunder, accomplishing nothing, exhausted, complaining of the rain.

Some enjoy abiding in drama more than they enjoy abiding in Christ, so much so that if they can't find the real thing, they will recycle it from the past, or create it on their own. Drama is an addictive drug, but it accomplishes nothing. Yet it does give the user something to complain about.

Or one can choose to live in the peace of Christ.

Where do you choose to abide?

February 17

There was a very wealthy, very devout man, who gave generously to his Church. As he began getting on in years, he started a bargaining process with God, in that, after loving God, the man loved his wealth ALMOST as much. Every night the man prayed "God, I ask you, may I PLEASE bring at least a portion of my wealth with me to heaven, when I pass?" For the first year, the answer was always "no." Finally, though, God took pity on the persistence of the man and told him that he could bring ONE SUITCASE with him to heaven. The man was overjoyed. He did his research and found that the most efficient means of transporting wealth is gold bullion. So he packed his suitcase with fifty gold bars. The next day he passed away.

The man arrived at the pearly gates, suitcase in hand. St. Peter stopped him and said, "Sorry sir, but you're not allowed to bring anything with you." The man stopped and said "Please check with God. He told me I could bring ONE SUITCASE filled with whatever I want. Peter checked, and came back and said, "Well, you're right. There's a first time for everything. Sir, if I might, can I take a look in your suitcase?" The man acquiesced, opening the suitcase to smugly show Peter all of the bars of gold. St. Peter looked thoughtfully, then turned to the man and said "Sir, one question—Of all you could have chosen to bring, why did you bring pavement?"

Value. On the surface, such a subjective thing.

Our society tells us, pressures us to value certain things: A linear career path, professional advancement, monetary reward, a large house, and an even larger 401-k—These things society tells us are of incredible value.

Yet we frequently give little thought to that which is of greatest value to God. Oftentimes, the things we value are intrinsically of no regard to God. Sadly, too, we often attribute no real value to those things most important to God. While we focus on what we can touch, feel, and measure, God values the intangible.

Matthew 22: 34-40

"Hearing that Jesus had silenced the Sadducees, the Pharisees got together. One of them, an expert in the law, tested him with this question: "Teacher, which is the greatest commandment in the Law?" Jesus replied: "'Love the Lord your God with all your heart and with all your soul and with all your mind.' this is the first and greatest commandment. And the second is like it: 'Love your neighbor as yourself.' All the Law and the Prophets hang on these two commandments."

Love.

What God values primarily is love—Love of God, and love of our fellow man, no matter how different they may be from us.

Where we want to quantify, God values the immeasurable.

What we need to internalize is that often what we call profit, God calls pavement.

February 18

We had a lot of kitchen fun this week! First, good breakfast sausages are hard to find in Mexico. SOooo, Glenda and I made six pounds of it on Sunday, from harvesting the sage and ginger from our garden, to grinding the meat, to stuffing the meat and spices into the casings. It was a rewarding day in the kitchen! Next, we started the process of making a prosciutto. This takes patience! First, one blends the spices. I used black pepper, paprika, garlic powder, and then the important stuff-- 3.25% of the weight of the meat in salt. We then rubbed the meat with the mixture of seasonings and salt and placed it in a vacuum-sealed bag, where it will cure at 55 degrees Fahrenheit, for about two weeks. Next, we will remove it from the bag, rinse off any of the remaining seasonings, and let it dry until it has lost 30% of its weight. While the garlic, pepper, and paprika have washed off, the salt instead has melted and permeated the meat.

This process of the salt permeating the meat is called "curing." What it does is preserve the meat, even at room temperature, in that it creates an environment where water is drawn out of the cells of toxic microorganisms via osmosis, thus killing the harmful microbes. The curing process also affects the texture of the meat itself. After curing and drying, the ham is now edible, but the flavor will improve with age. We've been lucky enough to taste fourteen-year-old prosciutto—At that age, the fats in the ham have become so tender that it melts in your mouth, as its melting point is now just 95 degrees. The meat, too, has a mellow smoothness to its flavor.

The transformation of a potentially dangerous cut of meat into a delicacy requires just two things: salt, and time.

Matthew 5:13

"You are the salt of the earth. But if the salt loses its saltiness, how can it be made salty again? It is no longer good for anything, except to be thrown out and trampled underfoot."

There are two key points I want to pull from this verse—In ancient times, people stored salt in cotton bags. If the salt was unused over time, the changes in humidity leached the sodium chloride from the salt, leaving just a white residue. If this happened, people cast that white powder on the streets, to keep the dust down.

Second, for salt to have a preservative effect, one must press it into the flesh, then give them time to interact for a prolonged period—The longer, the better.

Now here's the rub (every pun intended)—the Church encourages individuals to spend all of their available time doing "churchy" things. Sunday school, worship service, potluck dinner, Saturday prayer meeting, Saturday night bible study, Wednesday fellowship, choir practice... Then there is the code word vocabulary that one learns which further excludes those not in the church. Oh, don't forget about "Christian" schools, "Christian" colleges, "Christian" bookstores, coffee houses... This goes on with the result that over 90% of new converts to the faith from high school age on up lose or shun all of their non-believer friends within the first year of their coming to Christ. Basically, the church forces all of the salt into the salt bag with other salt, where time works to remove the saltiness of every grain.

And this is exactly the opposite of what Christ called us to do.

No, we are not to be of the world, but Christ directly commands us to be in it, instead of in some little "Christian" ghetto. We are SUPPOSED to press the flesh, and take the time in the world to make a difference, to not just preserve, but to bring flavor.

You are the salt of the earth. What flavor are you bringing to those around you?

February 19

Monday, Glenda, aka the Wild Love Monkey, and I were walking into our favorite pizza place. As we ascended the stairs, they were playing the Bee Gees on the sound system. I noticed that Glenda and I were each walking in time to the music.

I have a very eclectic taste in music. I love jazz, Elvis Costello's old punk days, Pink Floyd, Supertramp, Dire Straights, Queen, Foreigner, U2, R.E.M., Pussycat Dolls, Michael Jackson, and more. I also am moved by Handel, Mozart, and Bach. The one genre I dislike is country music. I don't mean to deprecate anyone who likes it, it's just not my thing. Oh, and for those who do like country music, to deprecate means to look down upon. JUST KIDDING! Borrowing an old Bob Newhart stand-up line... All jokes aside, I even like the Carpenters. I draw the line at The Captain and Tennille, though. But hey, the Carpenters did have some good lyrics...

"We've only just begun to live

White lace and promises

A kiss for luck and we're on our way

Before the risin' sun, we fly

So many roads to choose

We'll start out walkin' and learn to run

(And yes, we've just begun)

Sharing horizons that are new to us

Watching the signs along the way

Talkin' it over, just the two of us

Workin' together day to day..."

Believe it or not, I'm going to tie this all together... Consider this passage—

Romans 5:3-5

"And not only that, but we also glory in tribulations, knowing that tribulation produces perseverance; and perseverance, character; and character, hope. Now hope does not disappoint, because the love of God has been poured out in our hearts by the Holy Spirit who was given to us."

Now, I've got to say, that for decades the idea that "hope does not disappoint" has left me flummoxed, for I've had many hopes dashed upon the rocks. And then just the other night, thinking through the lyrics of the Carpenters' song above, and thinking of Glenda, it made sense: Hope that is based on Love and Truth does not disappoint.

I have hoped for a loving strong marriage with Glenda. That marriage has been based in Love and Truth. We have been together for 40 years now, and I can honestly look at her and say, "We've only just begun, to live, white lace and promises..." That is because our love began in eternity past, exists now in eternity present, and will continue into eternity future. We share new horizons and have explored new lands and ideas, and continue to do so, learning as we go. And yes, considering eternity future, we've only just begun.

And if that is the case with Glenda, especially understanding how fallible I am, imagine how it is with God.

The new day is here, and I must get going. I'll grab a kiss for luck and be on my way...

Have a great day!

February 20

Last words. It is very interesting to study the last words of honorable people. Groucho Marx, who dedicated his life to making people laugh and see the brighter side of life left with one last joke, saying, 'Well this is no way to live," as he exhaled his last breath. Leonardo Da Vinci said on his deathbed "I have offended God and mankind, because my work did not reach the quality it should have." George Orwell's last written words were "At 50, everyone has the face they deserve." He died at age 46. And Winston Churchill, NOT an honorable man, had last words showing his character, "I'm bored with it all."

It is too easy to overlook the true meaning of words, to cheapen them by misuse. I mean really, how can one "love" their toilet paper? As I think on this, there are some passages of scripture that terrify me. Psalm 139:23-24 is one—"Search me, God and know my heart; test me and know my anxious thoughts. See if there is any offensive way in me..." Wow. That is a prayer I don't know if I honestly dare to ask, as the act of having to face those offensive ways, my anxious thoughts, I know would undo me. Then there is Paul's statement, "Be imitators of me, just as I also am of Christ." Nope, I don't have the courage or the foolishness to say THAT to anyone either, because I own a mirror... Thankfully, these passages are descriptive, not prescriptive!

Then there were Paul's last words to his beloved disciple, Timothy:

2 Timothy 4:5-7

"But you, keep your head in all situations, endure hardship, do the work of an evangelist, discharge all the duties of your ministry. For I am already being poured out like a drink offering, and the time for my departure is near. I have fought the good fight, I have finished the race, I have kept the faith."

The word Paul used here, translated as "kept," has an intense literal meaning. The Greek "tereo" means "to watch over, to preserve." The word picture is then of a guardian. Paul, knowing his impending passing, said then of his life that he fought the good fight, finished the race, and was a guardian of the faith.

I would so love to be able to say that at the end of my days, but the truth is, I am so easily distracted. I mean really, this morning I was on Instagram, looking at cute pictures of dogs so intently that Chaucer, my English Setter, had to come over and bump my hand to remind me that there were three REAL dogs in the room with me, who love me and want some attention.

So today, I ask you to join me in querying yourself some very real questions—Namely, what would one watching your life assume that the object of your fight is? What is hindering you as you run your race? And what stands in your way of being a true guardian of the faith? It may be profitable to pair up with a friend to pray through these questions, but they are worth exploring.

February 21

A week ago today we adopted a Great Dane rescue, named Maya. Maya had been abused, then tied to a telephone pole, and left to starve. A rescue agency in Guadalajara stepped in and took Maya, who was welcomed by a wonderful couple nearby to foster her. In that they already had several dogs, all of them small, they needed desperately to place Maya in her forever home, and that's when we stepped in.

Although Maya weighs about 105 pounds, she is easily 30 to 45 pounds underweight due to her having been starved. We set up a feeding station for her in the front courtyard, but she wouldn't eat. Oh, we could hand-feed her some chicken or a hardboiled egg in the kitchen, but Maya, still in starvation mode, would not eat out on the courtyard.

Then Glenda had an epiphany: Maya had been traumatized by having been abandoned. Maybe, just maybe, she was afraid to eat outside, because she feared being abandoned again. We moved her feeding station inside, and BOOM! Maya began tucking into her food.

The trauma of abandonment affected Maya so intensely that she would have literally continued to starve herself to death rather than eat outside.

Trauma. The Oxford English dictionary defines trauma as "A psychic injury, especially one caused by emotional shock the memory of which may be either repressed and unresolved, or disturbingly persistent." Trauma is a kind of haunting, which Ann Laura Stoler defines as "to frequent, resort to, be familiar with...to be frequented by and possessed by a force that not always bears a proper name." A familiarity that will not leave...

Maya experienced a trauma that so wounded her that her fear of abandonment surpassed her need to eat.

Many of us deal with traumas because, as my friend Rod noted, "A child does not question the wrongs of grownups, he suffers them." Yes, the wounds caused by those in a position of power, especially in what should be a relationship of love and trust, run deep.

Maya's trauma will dissipate when she realizes that she has found her forever home, that she will never be abandoned again, and that means building trust and a bond of love.

Deuteronomy 31:6

"Be strong and of good courage, do not fear nor be afraid of them; for the Lord your God, He is the One who goes with you. He will not leave you nor forsake you."

When we understand that God will NEVER leave us or forsake us, well, my friends, that means that in Him we have our forever home. Understanding that, meditating on that, internalizing the reality of the Love of God which exceeds temporal bounds, well that, my friends, can be a HUGE step in each of us being able to move beyond our traumas.

Teddy Bears can help children with hauntings. The ever-present love of God is a healing balm to the traumas of adults.

As I write this, Maya is standing next to my chair, holding out her paw, a desperate gesture to know that she can be touched. And as I take it, this thirty-pound head lands in my lap.

And Christ holds out His hand to you…

February 22

Almost three years now since we expatriated to Mexico. They have been the happiest three years of our lives. We are faced with the challenges of learning a new language, fitting into a different culture, have had ¾ of our time here in pandemic mode, and have started a new business, and yet this has been the least stressful three years of our lives as well.

And the most productive.

I think one of the big factors is that we have ceased watching TV. Oh, we'll watch a movie, but nothing on commercial TV. We also don't listen to the radio--Hey, music fills the streets here, so why bother? It's amazing how well the advertising on TV and radio works. But with the absence of it, we are so much more at peace, so increasingly content not just with what we have, but also with who we are. We've had several friends here say that they came to Mexico to spend their last years, and die, but instead have learned how to live.

I know our lives have gotten so much bigger, more creative, and happy.

The two economic levers of the US economy are war and an advertising-driven sense of personal inadequacy that drives a consumer mentality, leaving room for little else in one's soul.

It is amazing how much societal expectations can make one's life smaller, along with one's perception of the world around them, as well as their idea of God.

Ephesians 3:16-19

"I pray that out of his glorious riches he may strengthen you with power through his Spirit in your inner being, so that Christ may dwell in your hearts through faith. And I pray that you, being rooted and established in love, may have power, together with all the Lord's holy people, to grasp how wide and long and high and deep is the love of Christ, and to know this love that surpasses knowledge—that you may be filled to the measure of all the fullness of God."

One of my favorite movies is "Joe Versus the Volcano." In one scene, the protagonist, played by Tom Hanks, has been adrift at sea for a long time. He watches the moon rise over the ocean, and says, in a weakened voice "Dear God, whose name I do not know, Thank you for my life. I forgot how...big." Then he passes out. It took his character time away from the things of man, to return to understanding God and His gift of life.

Paul's prayer here is that we "grasp how wide and long and high and deep is the love of Christ, and to know this love that surpasses knowledge—that you may be filled to the measure of all the fullness of God." I certainly have never fully grasped that degree of the fullness of God. However, with our move here it is clear that I sought for decades to fill my life with a lot of other things other than the measure and fullness of God.

And we are finite vessels. The more we fill our lives with wants, desires, anxieties, and insecurities, the less room we have for God. And Paul gives us the key to opening that full room for God, namely, being rooted and established in love. Not in cultural or societal norms, not in a "successful" career (whatever that is), not in popularity, but in love.

So the question is, where, really are you planted? What do your roots grow in to find nourishment?

February 23

Today is a fun day for me, as we're getting ready for another of Glenda's art shows. These are always nervous times for her, because she is the artist, and has the understandable fear that perhaps others will not like her work. They always do, so for me the day before the show is exciting, while for Glenda there is a sense of trepidation. Same show, two opposite reactions, a dichotomy.

Life is full of unexpected dichotomies. Consider this: sautéed Brussels sprouts are slightly bitter, and mustard powder is bitter. But if you lightly sprinkle some mustard powder on Brussels sprouts as they are sautéing, it removes the bitterness. Another dichotomous truth is that the more you learn, the more you understand how little you know. Then there is this—we live our lives forwards, but understand it backward.

One of the most poignant dichotomies is this: we all desperately want to be fully and intimately known, at least by someone. We want someone as a witness to our lives, our feelings, the sum of who we are. However, we all fear being fully known, because what if somebody sees THAT side? You know, the ugly or scary side of us, that part we don't even want to see, don't want to acknowledge. We want to be, yet fear being, fully known, understood.

Because, if anyone sees THAT side, the darkness, how could they love me, they will reject me...

And we all want, need to be loved, accepted.

Psalm 139:1-6

"O Lord, You have searched me and known me. You know my sitting down and my rising up; You understand my thought afar off. You comprehend my path and my lying down, And are acquainted with all my ways. For there is not a word on my tongue, But behold, O Lord, You know it altogether. You have hedged me behind and before, And laid Your hand upon me. Such knowledge is too wonderful for me; It is high, I cannot attain it."

John 15:9

"As the Father loved Me, I also have loved you; abide in My love."

My friend let this sink in: you are fully known, understood, comprehended by God.

Simultaneously you are also fully loved by God.

God is the ultimate witness to your life, and knows you more intimately than anyone else.

And God chooses to love you, just as you are.

In that is no contradiction.

If that doesn't set you up with a good start for your day, I don't know what will.

February 24

It seems to be in vogue these days in certain circles to continually post on social media about "only having time for those who make me feel good," and a host of other trite sayings about how everyone who is not in their lives anymore is in that "predicament" because it is THEIR fault. There is a word for those who only make one feel good, who will tolerate every bit of poor behavior without a word:

Enablers.

You see, real friends will call out bad behavior in your life. Through these actions, one confronts realities that they may not have seen before, and they grow. Enablers do not understand the difference between real friendship and attention-seeking. They are so worried that others may reject them that they will tolerate, excuse, and even encourage the worst of behaviors. Oh, they may make one feel good, but there is no nutritive value in that sickly sweet flattery they feed you.

I'm still friends with about 80% of my high school and college buddies. They have challenged me and busted my chops, as I have theirs, and we are still friends because even back in high school we were more adult in understanding relationships and the value of real friendship than many contemporaries I know.

Proverbs 27:17

"As iron sharpens iron, so one person sharpens another."

Proverbs 27:6

"Faithful are the wounds of a friend, but the kisses of an enemy are deceitful."

A true friend challenges you to be better, and does not blow smoke where it doesn't belong! There are many, many people out there who will try hard to force you into the role of an enabler, people who just want continual praise. And hey, praise is fun and makes us feel good, but it is destructive if not deserved. As "friendly" as a person might be to you, if they are filling your life with undeserved praises, they are actually your enemy.

It is a worthwhile endeavor to take stock of one's friend relationships from time to time. If someone is trying to mold you into being an enabler, walk away without a second thought, they are not your friend. If some offers you empty flattery, too, get that shoe leather going without regret. But the ones who challenge you, push you to be better, to seek and see the truth, even when it's painful, well they are worth their weight in gold. Hold on to them for all your worth. They will stand by you to the end. As John Lennon noted, "Being honest may not get you a lot of friends but it'll always get you the right ones."

February 25

I got new glasses yesterday!! YAY!! If you have very poor eyesight, like me, you understand that this is a big deal. For those who do not know the full experience, here's how it goes: one starts with perfectly good glasses. A year goes by, maybe two, and you notice no changes. Same with years three, four... Then, around year five, a scratch appears. It is, ironically, on what they call the "scratch-resistant coating."

The scratch-resistant coating is kind of like the Teflon on a frying pan. As long as it is all intact, great! But, once there is one scratch, the integrity of the coating is gone, and others appear. No, they don't appear, they multiply at night as evil gnomes, seeing the weakness, come in and inflict more and more damage on the lenses.

And then you say, "Wow, maybe I should get new glasses..."

And so you go to the eye doctor, have your exam, and lo and behold, not only are the lenses scratched beyond belief, but you need a new prescription as well, as your eyesight has changed.

So when the new glasses show up, it's like magic. You can see things you never knew you missed.

Or, you could have gotten your eyes checked each year, and gotten the prescriptions you needed when you needed them...

2 Peter 1:5-9

"But also for this very reason, giving all diligence, add to your faith virtue, to virtue knowledge, to knowledge self-control, to self-control perseverance, to perseverance godliness, to godliness brotherly kindness, and to brotherly kindness love. For if these things are yours and abound, you will be neither barren nor unfruitful in the knowledge of our Lord Jesus Christ. For he who lacks these things is shortsighted, even to blindness, and has forgotten that he was cleansed from his old sins."

There is a creep in one's shortsightedness that everyone who wears glasses realizes. Still, most of us wait for that "scratch-resistant coating" to start to deteriorate before we consider an examination

Same thing, too often, with our faith. Oh, we are good at building up our own scratch-resistant coating, holding to, adding assumptions that affirm what we have chosen to believe as "truth." Then, if we're lucky, something happens to disrupt the integrity of that veneer.

And our eyes grow ever more dim, until we take the time for self-examination, to test our assumptions, our beliefs.

So, take it from this shortsighted man—be diligent in that self-examination. Challenge your assumption. Check the facts.

Your foresight will improve dramatically!

February 26

My favorite job was being the college and young singles pastor at a Church in a Dallas, Texas suburb. I had effectively two bosses—The Senior Pastor, and the Youth Pastor, both of whom were great guys. The job started as an internship and became full-time. The young men and women in the class were, for the most part, intellectual sponges, who were a delight not just to teach, but to interact with as well. I still keep in touch with several of them, though my tenure there ended almost thirty years ago.

Yet no place is perfect. I remember a very sad incident, when a nice young couple, teaching, I believe, third-grade Sunday School taught the kids a song to help them learn about Moses. To the tune of "Louie Louie," the song when "Pharaoh Pharaoh, Whoa, Whoa, let my people go…" I thought it was kinda cute.

They got their butts handed to them.

For the life of me I couldn't figure out why, but the associate pastor made it very clear when I asked-- "They shouldn't be teaching that filth! That was the dirtiest song ever written!" I asked him what was bad in the lyrics, and he yelled at me, "I won't repeat that in the house of God!" And slammed the door to his office. About thirty seconds later, Roberto re-opened his door, sticks his head out, and yells, "Besides, children should be learning how to appreciate OUR music." He slammed the door again. He was a gifted slammer—did that at least once a day the whole time I worked there. But with that statement, he had let on to what his issue really was.

Ephesians 4:2-3

"Be completely humble and gentle; be patient, bearing with one another in love. Make every effort to keep the unity of the Spirit through the bond of peace."

The issue that Roberto and his cronies had with the song was simply this: they despised contemporary music (not that "Louie Louie" was immediately contemporary...) and wanted only old-time hymns in Church.

I think many of you know that I am way beyond not liking Country music. I really dislike it. BUT, when I was pastor of a Church in rural America, guess what? Most of the congregation LOVED country music. I remember one lyric in particular—"The devil's in the phone booth/He's calling 911/ Cuz he shaken in his boots when you pull out your spiritual Gu-Un..." Not something that appeals to one from my cultural and educational background. Heck, I was even yodeled at there once. But you know what?

There is nothing immoral or spiritually wrong with that style of music.

I just don't like it. But I encouraged it at our church, as it ministered to many.

To be humble, gentle, and patient, to bear with one another in love, implies that things are going on, styles, tastes, whatever, that we don't like, BUT are not in and of themselves wrong.

Roberto and his cronies, though, wanted what they wanted the way they wanted it—you know, Burger King style worship. And not knowing what love was, they did everything they could to keep worship only in the style THEY wanted. The internet was up and running then, they could have checked the lyrics, but they loved their prejudice more than they loved the truth.

And many left the church, in a slow trickle, including the nice Sunday School teachers who had introduced the song.

Oh, and "Louie Louie?" It was written in 1955 by Richard Berry, who was trying to capitalize on an influx of Calypso music. It is about a sailor looking forward to seeing his girlfriend In Jamaica. The Kingsmen re-recorded it, but there was a problem—The recording studio had only one microphone and it was suspended six feet in the air, and the electrician was on break. They had to gather under the microphone and record a virtually unintelligible version of the song. After complaints, the FBI even investigated, to see if there were any foul lyrics, to see if it should be banned from the airways.

There were none.

Let's bear with each other. No, we don't all like the same things, but trying to "spiritualize," or "moralize" the difference to make people behave as YOU want is just evil.

February 27

I LOVE the rainy season here in the mountains of Southern Mexico! It is in the nature of water to at least appear to yield, so each raindrop on one's cheek feels like a caress. Yes, one gets wet walking in the rain, but it is refreshing. The rain is patient, so that, even though the rainfall itself is gentle, the cumulative effect is amazing, as arroyos that have once been dry become rivers sometimes twenty feet deep and equally wide. And as gentle as water is, with a persistent flow, it will cut through stone.

Consider the Colorado River—Fifty feet wide, between ten to thirty feet deep, and yet its' constant flow carved the Grand Canyon, which is a mile deep, eighteen miles across, and two hundred seventy-seven miles long.

No, one raindrop may not do much, yet, though water always seems to yield, a constant flow accomplishes a great deal.

Galatians 6:9-10

"And let us not grow weary while doing good, for in due season we shall reap if we do not lose heart. Therefore, as we have opportunity, let us do good to all, especially to those who are of the household of faith."

The central courtyard in our house is paved with brick that is about fifty years old, and yet there are two bricks in a corner under an overhang of the roof where there is no gutter. They have eroded about an inch and a half down. Why? Because, during the rainy season, which lasts here for about four months, there is a constant trickle of water that lands on them during a storm. And here, it only rains at night. Not one drop caused a visible difference in the bricks. It was simply a constant, small trickle over fifty years.

Water needs no motivation; it is in its nature to flow. But we are humans, and sometimes yes, we get discouraged. But remember this, my friend, you are 70% water, and your heart even more so. Thus, if you remain persistent in doing good—feeding the homeless, finding homes for the stray dogs, loving those who seem so unlovable, well, my friend, your actions of love will cut a path into the hardest of hearts, and transform them into things of beauty.

Life is hard, and it is most difficult on those who seek to make a change, for it is those individuals who best see the inequities around them. And after years of trying to make a difference, one may feel that nothing has been accomplished. But your actions of love, applied with consistency, are among the most powerful things in this world.

One raindrop does not water a field, however, a full rainstorm will. So, let's join together in prayer to encourage each other to keep on going, and bring a downpour that will transform a dustbowl into a verdant garden.

The extraordinary does not come from the one-time epiphany, but from patient persistence.

February 28

Glenda and I were on the beautiful island of St. Lucia a few years back. We decided to splurge and rent a sailboat, with a captain, to sail around the island. It was a stunning craft—57' long, a wooden-hulled ketch. Glenda and I acted as crew.

The little inboard diesel Volvo engine gave us the power to get out of port, then we were under sail. The captain poured us each a rum punch. I was about halfway done with mine, and he poured himself another. A few more sips for me, and he poured himself a third. A few more kilometers down the coastline, and he was absolutely plastered, so I suggested we return to port. We didn't have much speed, and for some reason the captain chose to tack instead of jibe, turning us straight into the wind. The sail luffed, and we were dead in the water. "Take the wheel, Ted," he slurred. Gee, thanks!

There was a large wave coming, so I threw the wheel over hard, to use the waves' movement against the rudder to angle the boat sideways to the wind. It worked, and when the wind filled the sails, it was magical! The sails were full of sailboat fuel, the wooden hull vibrated as if with joy, and the boat leaped forward. The captain poured himself another rum punch...

Ephesians 5:18-20

"Do not get drunk on wine, which leads to debauchery. Instead, be filled with the Spirit, speaking to one another with psalms, hymns, and songs from the Spirit. Sing and make music from your heart to the Lord, always giving thanks to God the Father for everything, in the name of our Lord Jesus Christ."

We couldn't see the sailboat fuel, the wind, that filled the sails, but we did experience the effect! It is the same when our lives are positioned to be filled with the Holy Spirit—we are not just moved, but fully empowered.

Too often individuals seek the Spirit to gain a feeling, when the truth is, if we are truly filled, we are in motion, motivated to move on with a power that transcends us.

What is filling you today?

Congrats, you made it through the month!

Chapter Three

March

March 1

For all of us, there are times when it seems like we are at the lowest of lows. That feeling transcendent of sadness, where one feels hollowed out, not with a vacuum, which would pull something in, but with a capacity for only emptiness. I have been there: clinically depressed, I spent a weekend hospitalized in a psych ward. I was a senior pastor at a Church in Wisconsin then. When I returned, a group of the Church Elders could not stop gossiping about the event. I told them to stop or I would resign—They accepted my resignation, but reneged on our agreed-upon severance pay, because that's the loving thing that Christ would do. No, in reality, they got caught with their pants down as men without honor and wanted me out of that town as fast as possible.

It was a great valley in my life. Oh, sure, I've been through several valleys in my years, but that was the deepest. Yet, the current that flowed in that valley carved me in a new way. It took time to heal, but healing did come, resurrection even. I came out the other side a different man, but also a man who had learned an important lesson: when one is walking through the "valley of the shadow of death," the fundamental truth is that every shadow is cast by light. The existence of any and every shadow stands as incontrovertible proof of light.

Psalm 27:13-14

"I would have despaired unless I had believed that I would see the goodness of the Lord

In the land of the living.

Wait for the Lord;

Be strong and let your heart take courage;

Yes, wait for the Lord."

As dark as they may seem, valleys are places of immersion, baptism, of shaping. Time in the valley is never to be rushed. While it might not feel like it at the time, it is a place where healing, change, and growth takes place.

Yet for that to happen, we must do the hardest thing, which is to wait on the Lord.

God's timing is not ours, but He is seldom early, never late, and always on time to come to our aid. And healing does come; resurrection even.

We need to remember this: for every valley, there are two corresponding mountains—one that lies behind you, and the other that calls to you. When the river in the valley has re-shaped you, and when God has brought His healing to you, look forward to that other mountain, for it is yours to climb.

I shed a tear while typing this, not out of self-pity, but realization. A group on the Elder board for the Church I served sought to destroy me, and I have grown through the ordeal. They never will, and I pity them. Some people will strive to do the same to you, and succeed in hurting you. You will, in the long term, grow and thrive from the experience. The tormenters never will.

March 2

Back when I was in college, there was a large Southern denomination that forbade dancing. Even at their universities, no dancing was allowed, on or off-campus. The reason given? "It might lead to sex." Well, this inspired a lot of jokes. Here's one:

There was a young couple at this denomination's flagship university who were preparing to get married. They had diligently attended all pre-marital counseling sessions with their pastor and were at their last one. The young man asked, a gleam in his eye, "We've both been chaste for all of our lives. What about sex after we get married? Can we finally have sex?" "Of course," says the pastor, sex is a good thing within marriage in order to have children." "What about different positions?" asks the man. "No problem," said the pastor, "it's a good thing." "Doggy style?" "Sure," says the pastor, "no problem at all." "On the kitchen table?" "Absolutely." "Can we do it on rubber sheets with a bottle of hot oil?" "Enjoy," smiles the pastor. "Can we do it standing up?" "Absolutely not," admonishes the alarmed pastor. "It could lead to dancing."

It could lead to...

I doubt many fathom the damage done to the Church and the faith of individuals that this line of thinking has caused.

Genesis 2:16-17

"The Lord God commanded the man, saying, "From any tree of the garden you may freely eat; but from the tree of the knowledge of good and evil you shall not eat, for on the day that you eat from it you will certainly die."

Genesis 3:1-3

"Now the serpent was more cunning than any animal of the field which the Lord God had made. And he said to the woman, "Has God really said, 'You shall not eat from any tree of the garden'?" The woman said to the serpent, "From the fruit of the trees of the garden we may eat; but from the fruit of the tree which is in the middle of the garden, God has said, 'You shall not eat from it or touch it, or you will die.'"

Let's compare and contrast. All God said to Adam was "Do not eat from the tree..." But Adam, in communicating the command to Eve, added something "do not eat from it OR TOUCH IT..."

Because touching it might lead to...

When Eve touched the fruit, she didn't die. Therefore, it was an easy assumption for her to make that the whole commandment was false.

Let me say this very plainly: God's Word is good enough. We do not need to add to it, embellish it, to place upon it more rules and regs. There was a group in the Gospels who did that. They were called the Pharisees. Trust me, the story makes it clear that they were the bad guys.

"It might lead to" thinking deprives individuals of good pleasures. It also sets up a legalism that proves ineffective, and if that is fruitless, then, it is easy for many to think, the rest must be false as well.

I've been in ministry for over half my life, and every single child I've seen grow up in a household dominated by "It might lead to..." thinking has either left the faith or become a modern-day Pharisee. Not a good record of accomplishment.

Let us allow God's word to stand as is, and let us love God and each other enough not to add to it.

Who knows what that could lead to?

March 3

My wife and I were walking to our favorite French restaurant the other day, enjoying the sun and good conversation when BAM!! I heard a crash, turned to my side, and saw Glenda face down on the ground. A cobblestone had rolled out from under her foot and she fell. Amazingly, even though she caught herself with her hands and both knees, she was ok! A small cut on her hand, but that was it! We got to the restaurant, she washed her cut hand, we joked about it and went on with our conversation.

Funny thing is, I know a host of people who would have milked a fall like that for weeks...

John 5:2-9

"Now there is in Jerusalem near the Sheep Gate a pool, which in Aramaic is called Bethesda and which is surrounded by five covered colonnades. Here a great number of disabled people used to lie—the blind, the lame, the paralyzed. One who was there had been an invalid for thirty-eight years. When Jesus saw him lying there and learned that he had been in this condition for a long time, he asked him, "Do you want to get well?" "Sir," the invalid replied, "I have no one to help me into the pool when the water is stirred. While I am trying to get in, someone else goes down ahead of me." Then Jesus said to him, "Get up! Pick up your mat and walk." At once the man was cured; he picked up his mat and walked."

Jesus asked the invalid if he wanted to get well. The man didn't answer his question, but gave a dodge--"I have no help when the water is stirred..." An excuse, and shallow one (every pun intended) at best. Jesus saw through this—it is clear the man wanted the attention given to an invalid. Using the emphatic tense, which meant that this command must be done this instant, Christ ordered him to get up, get his mat, and walk.

There are some very needy people in this world. Individuals with legitimate requirements that transcend the norm. For instance, those who have suffered the trauma of loss that can take years for the raw pain to end. Then there are those who simply want to complain all the time about everything, milking it for all of the attention they can get—the Professional Very Needy Person (PVNP).

Don't be that person.

We all know them—the mom, who does nothing but complain about how difficult motherhood is, even though when she says such things she is wounding women who wanted children but could not have them. The guy who complains about his job constantly, but never sends out a resume.

And so it goes.

Here's a truth about pain: When a child cries, it is when the hurt has already happened, an event in the past. There may be residual pain, but the causal incident is over. Crying is the beginning of the process of being un-hurt. The chemical composition of tears includes both an antiseptic and an anesthetic. Their flow into the wound starts the healing process. It also draws the attention of an adult who can help.

Trauma brings a response, the response starts the healing process, and over time, healing takes place.

Unless you're a PVNP.

When you are wounded, yes, cry. But remember that those tears are for a past trauma that is already over, and that healing has already started.

And know that God hears those cries, and will attend. There is no room for excuses as to why one won't allow healing to take place.

March 4

Research. Ahhh, one of the most misused words on the planet! Like many things, lots of people think of it as an event, instead of a process. First, "research" is not about verifying a pre-existing assumption. It is, instead, about finding the truth, whether one LIKES that truth or not. I have multiple advanced degrees, including several Masters degrees, and a Ph.D. For both a Thesis and a Dissertation, the process begins like this: one conducts a literature review, where one first identifies all of the key books and articles written on the subject of interest in each relevant language. For the literature review itself, then, one writes a fifty to one-hundred-page document outlining the arguments of each of the key pieces you have identified. This then goes to your educated peers for review, to see if there are holes in your review. You amend your work; submit it again for peer review until the piece is deemed worthy. This process takes nine months to a year.

After the literature review is peer-reviewed and deemed worthy, then one develops his or her hypothesis, and identifies all relevant primary sources to look at. With the primary sources identified, the individual then writes a prospectus for research, which once again, you give to educated peers to review. This process takes another four to six months.

Then one begins the review of the primary source data, organizing it, and testing each piece against your hypothesis. Sometimes one's hypothesis must change during the process to fit the data. One NEVER tries to make the data fit the hypothesis. Then you write. A Master's Thesis will be about one hundred to one hundred and fifty pages, while a Dissertation will range from two hundred to eight hundred pages.

Or one can watch a YouTube video or listen to a talk radio segment that confirms one's opinions...

Proverbs 26:13

"A sluggard says, 'There's a lion in the road,

a fierce lion roaming the streets!'"

The deal is, that there is no lion... The sluggard is a fool. And fools make up their own "facts" to justify their behavior.

That's right, "Alternative Facts" are nothing new.

In this case, the fool is justifying staying at home, not going to work, and is hurting only himself, but that is not always the case. Consider this—My old college roommate posted at the height of the pandemic that the CDC called for an end to wearing masks. The problem is, that wasn't the case. I sent him a PM giving him the facts and links to the CDC and JAMA websites. He responded by texting "oops," but he left the post up for all to see, and for fools to believe, because it supported his un-researched opinion. At about the same time, I was involved in a discussion with a woman about issues of history. She said that A Ph.D. in history was worthless because one can get one in just two years. This, of course, is false, there is no two-year Ph.D. program in history in the world. But making up her "facts" allowed her to attempt to equate her YouTube "research" with the real thing.

Both of these individuals are fools, making up their own "facts," which are falsehoods, to bolster their ignorant opinions.

These are the type of people who choose their news networks based on their ideology, not their quality.

And in broadcasting these "facts," they are causing untold damage to the others foolish enough to listen to them.

In very rare circumstances some true research might agree with one's initial hypothesis. But the reality is, most of the time when real research reveals the truth, one must change one's hypothesis, one's thinking, to match the truth, instead of trying to adjust the truth to match one's thinking.

And the Truth shall set you free...

As uncomfortable of a process facing the Truth can be.

M arch 5

It is odd to realize that we share our house with three very large carnivores. I mean really, Chaucer weighs more than a lynx by ten pounds! Sassy comes in around seventy pounds, and Maya, who weighs what Glenda weighs, comes in at the size of a medium black bear. I remember watching our smallest dog one day hold a steel can on the ground with his paw and rip the can in half with his teeth. Steel, not aluminum. These carnivores are always unrestrained and sleep with us.

And we are not afraid, though any of them could kill us with one bite.

Though they are freakishly strong, with standard four-paw drive, with us they are always soft, loving, and gentle. They will rough house with each other, and it is a little disconcerting to see Maya, at about one hundred forty-five pounds, open her mouth and take Chaucer's entire head in her mouth (Chaucer is our English setter, about 60 pounds), but she never hurts him.

Despite their incredible strength, these saber-toothed kids define the word "gentle."

James 3:17

"But the wisdom that is from above is first pure, then peaceable, gentle, willing to yield, full of mercy and good fruits, without partiality and without hypocrisy."

Having dealt yesterday with some characteristics of a fool, In contrast, today I wanted to look at its antithesis, wisdom. And right there, the third word defining wisdom is the descriptor "gentle."

First, let's look at what gentleness is not. It is not weakness. Physical weakness, emotional, or character weakness signals a certain lack of ability. Gentleness is able. It is not passivity or wimpiness. The gentle person stands their ground when they know they stand for what is right.

The literal definition for the word used here, "Epieikes," is "Not insisting on the letter of the law, expressing considerateness that looks humanely and reasonably at the facts of the case."

Reasonably and humanely.

Wow.

And that, my friends, requires strength. To the point that I would say that gentleness is the apogee of strength, strength at its greatest form or height.

I do not mean just physical strength, though that can definitely be included, but strength, too, of intellect, character, of compassion. Gentleness is the bridle on the horse, which channels the massive energy of the animal to go in the proper direction.

Gentleness is the greatest demonstration of true power, of intensity rightly channeled for good.

I must go now, Maya has grabbed the armrest of my chair with her mouth and is trying to pull me across the room to play...

March 6

Maya, our rescue Great Dane, is starting to unwind and settle in. Chained to a telephone pole to starve to death for weeks, when we got her, she was friendly but very reserved. Now, she is a playful 145-pound puppy. As she's gotten used to us, we've sought to get to know her, to find out what she likes to do, and what she's good at. Sassy and Chaucer, our other two dogs, LOVE to chase balls. Maya, not so much, but she LOVES to play catch, and she's good at it! It just took a little time to get to know her, instead of imposing upon her the things we thought she should find fun.

Proverbs 22:6

"Train up a child in the way he should go, and when he is old he will not depart from it."

2 Corinthians 6:18

"I will be a Father to you, and you shall be My sons and daughters, says the Lord Almighty."

In the Proverbs passage, the literal translation of "in the way he should go" is "in the way, or manner he is bent." While many church lady types use this verse as an excuse for imposing a strict form of religiosity upon their children, that is not the meaning. Instead, the verse means that parents need to take the time to get to know their kids, and see how they are bent—that is, see what they are gifted at, and then encourage them to pursue those areas of giftedness.

Here's the problem: For a large swath of society in our culture, many parents construct a narrative of what their child's life should be like before that child is even born. What hobbies they should enjoy, what job they should pursue, what type of person they should marry, and the list goes on. They never take the time to get to know their kids, to see how they are bent, but instead, attempt to impose their narrative on their children.

And if the child (hopefully) rejects that imposed narrative, the parents believe the child is rejecting them, and so push him or her aside. That happened to both my wife and me.

When Glenda was sixteen, her stage band was invited to play at the Montreux jazz festival. Glenda played alto saxophone. Her parents never encouraged her to pursue music. In her freshman year at university, she excelled in her creative writing course, finishing at the top of her class. Her parents told her that she could not major in English, Art, or Photography, because there was no way to make money from them. Marrying me? I wasn't a doctor or a lawyer, so I was despised.

The thing is, Glenda's parents didn't reject her, they just never knew her, and couldn't imagine her not wanting to fit the narrative they had written for her life before she was even conceived.

If that has happened to you, I hope this gives you some sense of balance, of encouragement. Your parents didn't despise you, they just didn't know you, and rejected your denunciation of their imposed narrative. But healing is available, For God PROMISES to "be a Father to you, and you shall be My sons and daughters…" He can, and will re-parent you, just ask.

Glenda is now an internationally published award-winning photojournalist, and published author, and makes a good living as an artist. We just celebrated our 39th anniversary. I'm still not a lawyer or an M.D., though I am a doctor.

Oh, and if you are a parent, please take the time to get to know your children, to see how they are bent.

Must run, Maya is barking at me to play catch…

March 7

I know that this will sound like an anathema to many, but, when I was studying for my oral exams for my Ph.D., I stopped listening to the radio in my car. Every moment I was focusing on exam prep, running through book outlines in my head. It wasn't until this past week that I turned the radio back on, and that was by accident. Somehow, the car's Bluetooth system activated the playlist on my phone. Toto's "Girl Goodbye" came through the speakers.

Windows open on a beautiful day, I cranked up the volume.

Yeah, I was "that" guy…

I remember the night 47 years ago that Christ came into my life like it was yesterday. 47 years ago. The tenor of every emotion seemed to change. The next day, and for the rest of my life then on, one of the clearest ways that I can describe the experience is that the volume of my life was turned up. Way up. And every sound, every note, was so much clearer.

John 10:8-10

"All those who came before Me are thieves and robbers, but the sheep did not listen to them. I am the door; if anyone enters through Me, he will be saved, and will go in and out and find pasture. The thief comes only to steal and kill and destroy; I came so that they would have life, and have it abundantly."

Prior to Christ, my life was defined by "thieves and robbers," and I was emotionally bankrupt because of it. Then God turned the volume up. The thieves and robbers got drowned out. Now don't get me wrong—I'm sure not going to say "And now I am happy all the day," which is a trite lyric from a bad hymn. But I can say this—I began to, and have since experienced life abundantly.

Yes, there have been some times of ecstasy in abundance. There have also been times of deep sorrow. But in those times of sorrow, I could see even during the dark times that my faith in God was growing, as was my empathy, my compassion for my fellow man. And in that, on both sides of the pendulum swing, I have recognized life, and life abundantly.

Only a fool would despise the times of ecstasy, but, frankly, only a fool, too, would despise the times of sorrow, because that is where most of the growth in one's life occurs.

My friend, I wish you Life, and Life abundantly.

Oooh! "Bohemian Rhapsody" just came on in the other room! Time to crank up the volume...

March 8

In my studied opinion, I believe the halcyon days of American cuisine were in the late 1940s. Our troops, returning from Italy, Germany, France, and Japan, were bringing new recipes with them. I have the double-volume set of Gourmet Magazine's Cookbooks from 1947, and the inclusion of so many recipes from such different cultures is truly amazing, and some real fusion in both flavors and techniques started to take place.

Then came the 1950s with the post-war prosperity culture of convenience leading the way. The food became terrible, Jell-O became a salad, and recipes became "add a can of this, a packet of that put it in a casserole dish, a viola!

Tasteless "food" that took no time to make. In 1954, instant mashed potatoes were invented. They were so popular that neither my mother nor Glenda's knew how to make mashed potatoes from scratch. Oh, and my 1967 "Joy of Cooking" volume seems to be devoted to casseroles...

The nutritional value plummeted, with the instant mashed potatoes, as an example, having lost all of their dietary fiber, vitamin C, and beneficial minerals through the processing procedure. The trade-off? The sodium content went through the roof. Diabetes skyrocketed, as did heart disease.

Over the past decade, the US has started to make good headway in developing its own quality cuisine, but so much was lost as people grasped at convenience instead of quality.

Romans 12:9-10

"Love must be sincere. Hate what is evil; cling to what is good. Be devoted to one another in love. Honor one another above yourselves."

"Cling to what is good..." The word Paul used here, translated as "cling" meant literally "To be permanently glued to, adhered to."

Here's the deal: We often start in our faith with a great deal of zeal. We read scripture every day, engage in study, and set up partners to help stay accountable on memory verses and the like. All good things. And then the tyranny of the urgent tears us from the important. We let our own study time go, instead depending on authors to predigest the Word for us.

We call half an hour in the car listening to "Christian" radio as our "quiet time."

And we drift, losing our adherence to what is truly good, as our faith, our life, loses flavor.

And Jell-O becomes a salad...

But we can always return, and my challenge is for us to do just that.

So, my friend, Let's get cooking!

March 9

"They need to take care of this!" "Somebody needs to do something..." "Why isn't anyone taking care of..." The cries one hears every day, throughout the day. The problem is, those who wail these statements the loudest seem to constantly forget that we are all someone else's "They," "Somebody," "Anyone."

About six months ago, our gardener, Ernesto, called to say he couldn't make it the next day. Someone had stolen all of his tools out of his truck overnight. The next day though, right on time, Ernesto showed up, beaming ear to ear. As he had been calling his clients to apologize for not being able to work that week, one of them came over to his house, took him into Guadalajara to the Home Depot store there, and bought him a new mower, weed eater, blower, and two new gas cans.

The gentleman even filled up the gas cans for Ernesto on the drive back.

There was a job to do, many jobs actually, and this gentleman equipped Ernesto to do the needed work.

2 Timothy 3:16-17

"All Scripture is inspired by God and beneficial for teaching, for rebuke, for correction, for training in righteousness; so that the man or woman of God may be fully capable, equipped for every good work."

The word translated as "equipped" here means literally "to be completed, to have everything needed."

But isn't it easier to hope and complain about a "they need to..." than it is to step out in faith?

Unfortunately, many think of this verse as "equipping" in a negative sense. For instance, at a church I pastored in Atlanta, I showed up to an Elder board meeting to have my two most belligerent elders demand that I, "Preach against divorce!!" (One of these individuals was in a failing marriage). I said instead that I would teach on The Song of Solomon, which is God's sex and marriage handbook. NO! They wouldn't have it! They wanted to equip people against divorce!

But preaching against divorce is not equipping couples for a good marriage. Sure, it may have delayed a divorce or two, but it would not equip the people for a truly happy union.

Equipping is giving the person the tools they need for the job.

And God has given you those tools.

So if you are feeling passionate about something or seeing a need, that MAY just be a calling.

We are all someone else's "They," "Somebody," "Anyone."

Let's step to the plate, and not let them down.

M arch 10

I love seeing artists grow in their craft. Back in the late '70s, although I respected Billy Joel as a talented musician, I sometimes found him crude or crass. Now he is one of my faves. His wisdom and compassion have grown. A riff from one of my favorite songs goes "But the good old days weren't always good, and tomorrow ain't as bad as it seems…" Wise words.

We live in disturbing times, to be sure, and yet, unfortunately, a huge segment of society is basing their ethical, and ideological decisions on what they perceive as the biggest fears they face, and that is never wise. These people want to return to an idealized Shire, that never really existed, when the fact is, life cannot be lived moving backward, only moving forwards. There is a garden of paradise that ultimately lies behind us, but any attempt to return to it is met with certain death.

No, we MUST move forwards, we must progress, to the paradise ahead.

2 Timothy 1:7

"For God has not given us a spirit of fear, but of power and of love and of a sound mind."

When one bases a decision on a spirit of fear, that person must understand that God was not in that decision. There are four constants in this world: Taxes, death, change, and the Love of God. To say that any of these are not immutable is to live in the ignorance of a fool.

Yet there are some, a great many, actually, who seem to fear change even over death.

And making their decisions based on that fear, they make choices devoid of God. Wanting to return to an imagined Shire of the past, they champion that which is vulgar, unfaithful, dishonest, uncompassionate, and cruel.

And they do so by calling it "Christian values," because they will not trust God, but yield instead to fear, and their desire to return to the imaginary "good old days" of the past that never truly existed.

In so doing they mock true conservatism, which embraces that one must make progress, that we must move forward, but seeks to regulate the pace of change for the good of society.

In the Lord of The Rings Trilogy, there is a line that many casual readers skip over, but that many literary critics see as central to the story. Frodo and Sam have finished their task, against all odds, and through much pain. Sam the Brave says to Frodo that he is grateful for the chance to return home. Now here's the line—Frodo replies simply "There is no real going back." The crux of this line is twofold: The events of their lives have changed Frodo and Sam, and frankly injured them irreparably this side of Heaven. Also, of equal importance, the Shire, too, has changed, and will never again be the Shire of their memories.

And Frodo and Sam MUST be willing to adjust to the changes, if they are to survive, much less thrive.

Yes, return they can, to a geography, but culturally it will be to a different place, leaving the fear of their task behind them.

Friends, there is no Christ in fear, in a desire to go back. But we can in humility trust Christ to mold us into tools He can use to shape a new tomorrow.

That tool may be a forge, it may be a whetstone, or it may be something else, but He is able.

So fear not, and trust in the Lord with all of your heart, mind, soul, and strength...

And keep moving forward.

March 11

Confession time, I'm a Sci-Fi junkie. Star Trek, Lost in Space, Avatar, Alien, Stranger Things, I liked the first two, maybe three Star Wars, but then they lost me. Still, I like most Sci-Fi.

There are some unanswered questions in most Sci-Fi films, like, if you're traveling at warp speed and you turn on your headlights, what happens? Still many of the tropes are constant. One that is universal is this: if a person travels back in time, and makes even a small change, then there are HUGE repercussions back in the present time.

I think most people understand that. Make a change in the past and the ripples spread into the future, back to what is the present, changing the course of history. I mean, Marty McFly ran over a pine tree in Back to the Future, and the name of Twin Pines Mall changed to Lone Pine mall, right?

Hebrews 13:1-3

"Keep on loving one another as brothers and sisters. Do not forget to show hospitality to strangers, for by so doing some people have shown hospitality to angels without knowing it. Continue to remember those in prison as if you were together with them in prison, and those who are mistreated as if you yourselves were suffering."

I LOVE how the unnamed author of this letter starts each sentence: "Keep on," "Do not Forget," Continue..." The author is proceeding with the assumption that all who read this text are already doing these things—A very gracious supposition.

Here's the point: We all know that a little deed done in time travel past can have ripple effects to change the future, right? Why then do we so seldom realize that small acts of kindness now will change not just today, but also mold the shape of eternity?

Every choice we make, every single one, on how we treat someone else does two things: it makes this world a more heavenly or a more hellish place, and it shapes our souls into that of a more heavenly or a more hellish creature.

"The needs around me are so great, what can I do that will make a difference?" You can smile at your server and tell them how much you appreciate their attentiveness over lunch. You can take the beggar's hand in yours when you give them money because there is healing in the human touch. You can choose a parking place a few spaces away because someone who isn't as able-bodied as you might need it.

And the ripples of your actions will reach heaven, and your choices will reshape your soul.

As well you will make someone smile, maybe make their day, their week, their month…

So, "Keep on," "Do not Forget," Continue…," and you WILL be the change that this world needs.

March 12

Probably the best memory I have resides in the heart of one of the worst times in my life. On her birthday, about twelve years ago, Glenda received a diagnosis of cancer. Her mother had died, ultimately, from the treatment for the same type of cancer. My mother, too, was losing her fight with the same disease. I was numb: this was Glenda—the light of my life, the one person I know whose soul makes everything she touches more beautiful.

Cancer.

I'd been a pastor long enough to know that the fight to defeat the disease requires a team effort. I passed the word around among my history department colleagues at the University of Colorado, and to our friends in the neighborhood—A surprise party for Glenda—We'd watch and participate in the sing-along version of Mamma Mia. Our house was tiny, but about sixty people showed up. Wine flowed liberally, but this being our great neighborhood in Colorado, we were left with more wine after the party than we had when it started. The food ran out, and someone ordered more and paid for it themselves.

And we sang. Speakers turned up to almost full volume, and we sang and danced. Everyone danced in unison to the music of the movie with such enthusiasm that pictures literally began to fall from the walls. At 2:30 in the morning, when the last person left, Glenda turned to me and smiled, and said "I can do this now, I'm ready to fight." We both slept that night with the deepest gratitude paving the way to true rest, body, mind, and soul.

She has been in remission for more than a decade now.

Colossians 2:6-7

"Therefore, as you have received Christ Jesus the Lord, so walk in Him, having been firmly rooted and now being built up in Him and established in your faith, just as you were instructed, and overflowing with gratitude."

To say that I overflowed with gratitude for that night is an understatement, but that was also in the worst of times. There just comes a time when one can make a choice, a choice to be grateful, despite, in contradiction to, one's circumstances.

You see, God's character is immutable. His character and His love for us never wanes no matter the circumstances, no matter what we may do to screw up. And if we truly know that, believe that, then gratitude to God is utterly transcendent of circumstance.

My friend, if you are going through hell, and need someone to stand by you, ask. Others will join with you in prayer through the dark time. But remember this—God has not changed, and is still actively involved in loving you where you are, as you are.

March 13

Mechanized warfare began with the Gatling Gun, invented in 1862, and used to a limited degree in the civil war. It expanded with the Boer war, with the first fully mechanized war being WWI. Before that, the most formidable weapon for close combat was the broad sword, a weapon used from before Roman times, up to the mid-1800s. What made the broadsword such an effective weapon was that it had two edges so that it cut both ways.

In the West, we have sought to tame God. All too often He is portrayed as a cosmic vending machine. Pump in the proper coinage of prayerful verbosity, and we can manipulate Him by our "faith" into giving us the (usually material) desires of our hearts. He is cuddly in our portrayals, but as C.S. Lewis noted correctly of Aslan, "He is not a tame lion..."

Proverbs 9:10

"The fear of the Lord is the beginning of wisdom, and the knowledge of the Holy One is understanding."

No, we do not portray our God as fierce, but He is, and to fear, or revere (literal translation is to "understand the awesomeness, to revere") the Lord is the beginning of wisdom—Understanding WHO we are dealing with, and that no, He is not a tame lion, but the creator master of all of the universe is crucial.

That is one razor-sharp edge of the sword...

Another misnomer often taught in the West about God is that He is distant. The cosmic watchmaker who set into being the machinations of the world and galaxy, wound it up, and left. Oh, sure, He might look in once in a while, but He is distant, or so emotionally weak that he just craves our adoration and service.

Matthew 20:26-28

"It is not this way among you, but whoever wants to become prominent among you shall be your servant, and whoever desires to be first among you shall be your slave; just as the Son of Man did not come to be served, but to serve, and to give His life as a ransom for many."

Service is an intimate act. To serve well, one must understand an individual, and his or her needs, and then care about them enough to try to meet those needs. One cannot serve from a distance or truly serve without a sense of passion.

And Christ came to serve us.

This is so crucial to an understanding of Christianity that I will say without hesitation that if one does not know Christ as his or her servant, then one does not truly know Christ.

And that is the other razor's edge of the broadsword.

It cuts both ways...

And to understand in balance, it is not contradictory, but necessary to have that healthy, bowled-over sense of awe and reverence when dealing with God, but is also necessary to grasp that if we claim to know Christ, we must know Him as our servant, which, if understood correctly, increases that sense of awe, of reverence.

The Grace of God is free, my friends, but that does not mean it is cheap.

And no, He is not a tame lion. For those who have been so frighteningly blessed to hear His roar, that is more than abundantly clear.

March 14

As I sit at my desk and type, I'm looking out of my office window at our casita (guest house) and at the huge lime tree that towers over it. This is very unusual because lime trees are usually small, with most of them being about twelve feet in height. This tree is a good 25 feet tall. It produces fruit seasonally twice a year, while most lime trees produce only once annually, and many of the limes from our tree are the size of small oranges. And, oh my gosh, when it is in bloom, the air smells divine!

There are a couple of reasons for the vigor of this tree. First, frankly, we live in a volcano crater, and the volcanic soil is a near-perfect medium for plants. Second, in the mountains of South Central Mexico, there are a lot of rainstorms, usually three or four a week, almost always at night.

Psalm 1:1-3

"Blessed is the person who does not walk in the counsel of the wicked,

nor stand in the path of sinners, nor sit in the seat of scoffers! But his delight is in the Law of the Lord, and on His Law he meditates day and night. He will be like a tree planted by streams of water, which yields its fruit in its season, and its leaf does not wither; and in whatever he does, he prospers."

The rainstorms here in the mountains are not just sprinkles that water the plants; they are windy deluges, which shake all of the trees to their cores. It ends up, for a tree to be healthy and have a good root system, it requires storms, for as the wind shakes the tree, it pulls on the root system, stressing the smaller roots. As a result of this stress, more roots grow in the affected area, which then both provides more stability for the tree and also gathers more water to nourish it.

To the root of the issue, we need to endure storms if we are to be firmly planted.

Now, we do not need to seek out storms, they will come on their own, but when they do, we can take comfort in knowing this: not only are we getting nourishment, but our roots are growing deeper, adding more stability to our future life.

Another thing I love here is that the Psalmist makes it clear that the tree does not bear fruit constantly, but there is seasonality to it, and that is true in our lives as well. If you tend to have workaholic tendencies (which are NOT healthy...) like me, those periods when you don't see any fruit from your efforts can be very frustrating. Yet, those periods do not mean one is feckless; it is just the result of the natural seasonality of life. Keep at it, and you will see fruit, in its season.

Our lime tree has endured thirty years of storms. Instead of bearing fruit only once a year, it bears fruit twice a year in abundance each time.

My friends, having endured your storms, know that in season you will bloom, and all will gather to take in the aroma. Then the season for fruit will arrive!

March 15

I'm writing this on International Dog Day! Glenda and I have had dogs our entire married life together. In fact, we had a dog when we were just engaged. They have always been what people considered big dogs. Chaucer, our smallest right now, is about 55 pounds. Sassy, our Golden Retriever, is about 65 pounds. Rogue the Dogue, who passed away this year, was close to 70 pounds. We have done fieldwork and conformation work with our pups, so we felt like we knew dogs, especially big ones, pretty well.

Then two months ago we adopted a Great Dane rescue, Maya.

At 145 pounds plus, Maya has been a game-changer in our understanding of big dogs. If you are petting her, and start to walk away and she wants to be petted more, she will stand on your feet, locking you in place. You know how most dogs will kind of flip your hand when they want to be petted? Maya is big enough and strong enough that she will do that with your head when she wants you out of bed. Oh, and she thinks she's a lap dog, so before you sit on the couch, be sure to use the bathroom, as she will sit on your lap and you will not move until she wants to get down. Suffice it to say that our understanding of big dogs and the average size of our dogs has, um, grown through new experiences.

Ephesians 3:16-19

"I pray that out of his glorious riches he may strengthen you with power through his Spirit in your inner being, so that Christ may dwell in your hearts through faith. And I pray that you, being rooted and established in love, may have power, together with all the Lord's holy people, to grasp how wide and long and high and deep is the love of Christ, and to know this love that surpasses knowledge—that you may be filled to the measure of all the fullness of God."

To be rooted and established in love means to be growing in the medium of Christ. It is to experience in a real, tactile fashion His love. As any plant is rooted and established it does not remain static, but grows. Similarly, it is expected that we are to continue to grow in Christ, not to remain static, not just pew warmers, but doers, people with, and acting on, power—the power of Christ.

In so doing, we begin to understand the breadth and depth of the Love of Christ, as that love that surpasses knowledge fills us.

The short of it is, the more we truly experience our relationship with Christ, the more our understanding of Him, of His Love grows.

But that does not happen if we simply remain static.

Did Glenda and I have a good bit of experience with large dogs, and know them well? Yes. But that did not mean that our experience could not, should not still grow.

The funny thing is, the closer one gets to God, the more one realizes how far we are from Him. But the more we experience Him in new ways, the more we can comprehend the height, breadth, and depth of His Love, and act on that to the benefit of others.

March 16

One of the things I love most about living in Mexico is the country's love of art. You see it everywhere. Murals, which one sees around the world, are particularly plentiful in Mexico. Heck, people even paint the telephone poles! There is one art form though that I've only seen here—The Catrina doll. Now the emblem of every Day of the Dead celebration, the Catrina doll originally was a very dark reference. The dolls are of impeccably dressed, bejeweled skeletons. The image originated in 1910, when Jose Guadalupe Posada, a nationally renowned illustrator published the image of an upper-class Mexican woman wearing all of the latest

European fashions and jewelry, except the woman was just a skeleton.

Posada's rendering made the statement that the upper class of Mexico, though fabulously wealthy, were dead inside, and fed off of the poor. Others grasped his image and began to spread it, one being a famous mural in Mexico City, by Diego Rivera, in 1913. The original Catrina image helped inspire the 1911 Mexican revolution, and Rivera's mural added fuel to the fire. Each artist sent a clear message: the affluent, the ruling class, as fashionable as they were, were already dead.

And Jesus made the same statement about the ruling class, the Pharisees, in His generation, calling them "whitewashed tombs."

Today, the same descriptors are valid with huge swaths of the Church in America.

2 Corinthians 3:17-18

"Now the Lord is the Spirit; and where the Spirit of the Lord is, there is liberty. But we all, with unveiled face, beholding as in a mirror the glory of the Lord, are being transformed into the same image from glory to glory, just as by the Spirit of the Lord."

After a brief discussion with a former High School friend, he spat the words at me "Man! You've changed!" my reply was simply, "Yes, we are supposed to."

This issue here is, that if we are truly interacting with Jesus, with the Spirit, we are being transformed. And one cannot be transformed and stay the same!! That is true of the individual believer, and the Church. As society, its values and needs change, we as individuals and corporately as the Church must change to follow Christ's leading, and to meet the changing needs of those around us.

However, many call themselves "Christians," and many organizations that call themselves "churches" resist any change at all. They demand the same music and try to force the contemporary culture to mirror what they were used to in their time some thirty or forty years ago.

There is no way these individuals or "churches" can claim that they are being actively transformed from glory to glory...

How, my friend, have you changed over the past few years? How has your church, its outreach, its worship, and its music changed? If there has been no transformation, is there legitimacy to that faith?

Words to ponder.

March 17

I am SO PROUD of Chaucer Chaucer Puppy Bosser, our English Setter pup. He is such a thoughtful dog! Last night, Sassy, our Golden Retriever, was having a bad dream. Chaucer nudged my cheek with his nose, to awaken me. Upon waking, I heard Sassy whimpering in her sleep, and called to wake her. She woke, stopped crying, and went back to sleep. Chaucer kissed my cheek, tucked his head under my chin, and also surrendered to slumber. Earlier this week, out on the parapet directly off of my wife's studio, Chaucer went on point. He barked to get Glenda's attention; there on the parapet floor were two baby birds who had been blown out of their nest by a storm. Now Chaucer is a bird dog, and yet he did nothing to harm the babies—He just got Glenda's notice, so she could return the babies to their nest.

Chaucer is always looking out for everyone else. This time last year, Glenda and I were downstairs. Chaucer came tearing into the room, barked with great urgency, and then deliberately went behind me, pushed me towards the staircase, and ran up the steps. I followed, and he ran back out of our bedroom grabbed my hand with his mouth, and pulled me into the room. Rogue the Dogue, his fourteen-year-old brother, was in the middle of a heart attack. Chaucer had just saved his life.

Colossians 3:12

"Therefore, as God's chosen people, holy and dearly loved, clothe yourselves with compassion, kindness, humility, gentleness and patience."

Paul, building the reader's sense of self-esteem, leads here by reminding us who we are, "chosen," "holy" (meaning "set apart), and "dearly loved." He then uses a very unusual verb tense for the word "clothe," the aorist imperative, which translated means "You must now, IMMEDIATELY cloth yourself!" In other words, "You're naked! Get some clothes on!" He then outlines what the specific items of clothing are: "compassion," "kindness," "humility," "gentleness," and "patience." Not exactly the armaments for a zero-sum conflict, but absolutely needed if one is to live in a healthy community.

And a healthy community will always accomplish so much more than a person endowed with "rugged individualism."

It is exsanguinating to me, though, that Chaucer, my dog, acts with more empathy, more compassion, than many humans I know. In saving his brother's life, Chaucer put Rogue's needs ahead of his. In choosing to point out the baby birds, Chaucer suppressed his predatory instincts. In awakening me to care for Sassy, again, he put his sister's comfort ahead of his own.

He made deliberate choices, each of which went against his instinctive nature.

We are called to do the same, make choices against our nature, for the better sake of the human community.

So whatcha wearing today?

March 18

This is the third old house we've renovated, and it is by far the oldest, with a portion being 400 years old. One thing each old house that we've renovated has had in common, though, is that the wiring is always...suspect. About a year ago, we had two ceiling fans installed in the dining room and the living room. They fit well with the contemporary Mexican feel of our house, and each had its remote control to adjust the fan speed and turn on and off the light. And they were awesome!

Until they weren't.

About six months ago, one of them stopped working entirely. I got new batteries for the remote, but nothing. Then last week, the other one ceased operation. "Great!" I thought, "We're going to have to have the whole system rewired!" Streams of pesos danced in my head, then Tuesday, I came home from the market, and both lights were on! The remotes worked for the fans as well! I pointed it out to our housekeeper, Bertha, who laughed and pointed me to two switches on the wall that I never thought connected to anything (very common in older homes that have been re-wired many times). The fans and remotes worked just fine, I simply had to turn the power on...

Ephesians 1:18-21

"I pray that the eyes of your heart may be enlightened in order that you may know the hope to which he has called you, the riches of his glorious inheritance in his holy people, and his incomparably great power for us who believe. That power is the same as the mighty strength he exerted when he raised Christ from the dead and seated him at his right hand in the heavenly realms, far above all rule and authority, power and dominion, and every name that is invoked, not only in the present age but also in the one to come."

In our walks with Christ, we often focus much more on the future, which we call "eternity" than the present. But the fact is, we are living in eternity present, and we possess "his incomparably great power for us who believe" NOW. Too often though, we fail to act on it.

We forget, as I did to turn the switch on, or that there is even that power available, but the power is there...

Just from this passage, we see that those who know Christ have a reason for hope, have a glorious inheritance, have incredible power IN THIS PRESENT AGE, and also in the age to come.

So if you really internalize that, make it yours, what is holding you back?

Have a great day! Power up!

March 19

We love the hummingbirds here, and they are quite tame. The flowers in our garden draw them, but the flowers aren't always in bloom, so, as we have several hummingbird nests on our property, we realized that we had a stewardship responsibility to care for them. That is why we set up feeders. The same thing with the Monarch butterflies—we are just a couple hours away from where they over winter, directly in their flight path, so we planted milkweed, their food of choice.

To be a steward is, literally from the meaning of the Greek word, to manage a house or estate that is not one's own. God put in our path the hummers and the Monarchs, so we care for them, though we do not own them.

God places people in our paths as well.

The phrase "One Another" is used in the New Testament 100 times. In the original Greek, it is one word, "alleleon." Fully one-third of the times it is used, it means this:

John 13:34-35

"A new command I give you: Love one another. As I have loved you, so you must love one another."

I won't bore you with all of the other proof texts, because the meaning is clear. The verb tense is the imperative. This is not a suggestion. Love is a verb, and we are called to love one another, even if we don't have much in common. Even if the other person doesn't share our sense of style, wit, or taste in music, you name it.

I was on the pastoral staff of a church when I witnessed a young woman carrying a baby come into the church office. She asked the secretary for a few dollars so she could get breakfast for her son. The secretary said, "I'm sorry, we don't keep cash here." I knew this was a lie, as we kept a cash box for emergencies, and I'd seen the secretary give cash to some of her friends who were short for a day or two. I darted out and gave the woman $5.00, then returned and challenged the secretary. She said tritely, "Give a man to fish and he eats for a day, teach a man to fish and he eats for a lifetime." She, of course, had done neither, but it made her feel better to say the words.

NO, dammit, NO! When another human in need comes by your path, your job, pure and simple is FISH! Get them what they need then! After that, if you have the means, sure, buy a rod and reel and lures, and take your time to teach them to fish. But when the immediate need is fish, your job, your stewardship responsibility is FISH.

As I'm writing this, I just got a text from a friend whose husband has acute covid, and needs hospitalization, and wants to see if I can help her set up a go fund me page, as they are out of cash. My job now is fish, so I must sign off.

Loving one another means we are responsible one to another, not to judge somebody's previous choices, but to meet the need now.

Every person you see is an image-bearer of God and deserves as such to be loved, so set the excuses aside, and fish...

March 20

I received a very poignant email from my friend Ted Fahy this weekend. Ted is an MD and was sharing with me some of his thoughts on where the spiritual and the practice of medicine intersect. He shared a chapter from a book one of his colleagues had written, in which she quoted him several times. This is one of those quotes: "Well", he said, "a physical exam is a sacrament. The gentlest touch when examining a kid with a very sore throat is a sacrament. I don't always need to touch them at all, once I have the rapid strep screen in my hand, but I do, because it's important. That light touch when they are hurting, being careful not to hurt them more, is a sacred act between doctor and patient. How you touch a patient in the exam room is a sacred rite. It is the laying on of hands, a sacred healing." I think Ted is spot on.

Sacrament.

How we have made that such a politically charged word of exclusion.

The definition of a "sacrament" is this: "A religious ceremony or act regarded as imparting spiritual grace to the participants or having spiritual benefits (source, Oxford English Dictionary). I say we have made this exclusionary in that in much of Christendom, we have chosen to limit the imparting of a sacrament to a priestly class, when this is antithetical to scripture.

1 Peter 2:5

"You also, like living stones, are being built into a spiritual house to be a holy priesthood, offering spiritual sacrifices acceptable to God through Jesus Christ."

1 Peter 2:9

"But you are a chosen people, a royal priesthood, a holy nation, God's special possession, that you may declare the praises of him who called you out of darkness into his wonderful light."

Yes, there is an ongoing effort—We are in the process of being built together, that is to stand in unison in purpose, but positionally now we are "a holy priesthood," "a royal priesthood." With that, we have the responsibility to "offer spiritual sacrifices acceptable to God through Jesus Christ," and to "declare the praises of him who called you out of darkness into his wonderful light."

The understanding of our roles as priests is a lacuna in the thinking of most believers, yet it is an identity that is real.

We all then, each one of us, are to extend sacraments, that is, acts of spiritual grace, to impart spiritual benefits, to this world.

And that can, if approached properly, look like a hug. A smile to one who is lonely. A kind word to one discouraged, the sacrifice of one's time to help someone in need. The list goes on.

And when we do that, two things happen. First, the recipient of that grace, that sacrifice, that kindness, have the opportunity to see a new facet of God. Second, we ourselves become slightly more holy. Holy, another word that we have often changed to mean "one of THOSE people, you know over there, made of unobtainium..." But in its actual meaning, it simply means "to be set apart." In this context, to be set apart unto God.

So the more we take on our priestly mantle as individuals and deliver the sacrament of love, of sacrifice, of healing to this world, the more we realize our being set apart unto God.

And you don't even need to own a robe...

Ted Fahy identified a sacrament in his work. In my work, in part, I write these, and try to provide quality, healing rest to people in need through our inn. Take a moment and meditate—What can you do you now, or what can you transform into a sacrament in your daily life? As Martin Luther noted, "A milkmaid can milk cows to the glory of God."

Sacrament.

How we understand God and how we approach life determines if we are delivering a sacrament.

March 21

Dog doors are wonderful things! When we moved down to Mexico, our friend Michael connected us with a GREAT ironworker names Jesus. The house already had wrought iron doors, but none of them matched, and you know me and symmetry... Jesus designed three BEAUTIFUL matching doors, a matching gate, and in the door to the backyard he put in a cleverly disguised dog door.

Rogue the Dogue took to it instantly, and Chaucer learned within one day. THEN there is Sassy. Sassy will go out of the dog door with no problem.

However, she refuses to come back in through it, and we've been here three years.

Even Maya, our Great Dane rescue, learned to use the dog door. She was SO proud of herself the first time she used it that she spun around at least ten times, then ran in place for almost a full minute—A very cute sight to see with a 145-pound dog!

But Sassy... She will stand there and bark and bark to come in, like there was a wall between her and us, though she had just let herself out a few minutes earlier. And her separation anxiety mounts...

Romans 8:38-39

"For I am convinced that neither death, nor life, nor angels, nor principalities, nor things present, nor things to come, nor powers, nor height, nor depth, nor any other created thing will be able to separate us from the love of God that is in Christ Jesus our Lord."

When Sassy is on the other side of the dog door, there is no real barrier between her and us, as she knows how to use the door. She does have, however, some kind of an imagined barrier that separates her from us.

I could get frustrated with her, but truth is, often I'm not that different.

Paul's exhaustive list makes it very clear that nothing, NOTHING can separate us from the love of God, which is In Christ Jesus.

But I make stuff up and imagine that there is a barrier between me and the love of God.

Usually, that has to do with how I perceive my behavior, thinking that somehow, I am not worthy of love. But, God's love glows in Grace, that is unmerited favor. And that's a game-changer.

I hear the question asked often of, "What would you do if you knew you couldn't fail?" An interesting question, but a more important one to ask is "What would you do if you knew you would always be loved?"

Now that is not just inspiring, but it is also the truth.

Nothing can separate us from it.

Gotta run, Sassy's barking at the back door...

March 22

In 1997, Air Force Captain Amy Svoboda was one of only 14 female Air Force fighter pilots, and she was good at her job. On a moonless night, piloting an A-10 attack aircraft over the desert in Arizona, Captain Svoboda finished her practice bombing run. Receiving orders to pull up and return to base, she accelerated, pulled up, and slammed into the ground at over four hundred miles per hour.

With the aggressive maneuvers and g-forces pulling at her from multiple directions, Captain Svoboda did not realize she was flying upside down.

I echo the thesis of Dallas Willard that a huge portion of "Christendom" in the United States is doing the same thing.

There is significant confusion in the States as to what Christianity is. First, I will start with what it is not. It is not a default position. Too many times I've heard people say, "Well, I'm not a Muslim, a Jew, or a Buddhist, so of course, I'm a Christian." No. Being a Christian involves a personal, real choice, not a default setting.

The second major confusion point—one often propagated from thousands of pulpits, is that Christianity is an ethical or moral system. "Jesus is all about being against sin!" Well, considering his best friends were prostitutes, tax collectors, and revolutionaries, it's hard to get traction with that.

And here's the deal—When confronted with the law, Christ always raised the bar to an impossible level. Many read the Sermon on the Mount and think "What a beautiful moral lesson." No! Christ is telling people that "Do not commit adultery" means you can't even look at someone with lustful intent without being guilty of infidelity. Oh, and if you are angry with your brother, heck, you're already guilty of murder! Forgiving somebody seven times is enough? No! Seventy times seven times is still not good enough!

And the list goes on. Why?

Because Christ is showing us we can't do it.

Because no one who thinks they can save themselves will seek out, or accept the offer of a savior.

Ephesians 2:8-9

"For by grace you have been saved through faith; and this is not of yourselves, it is the gift of God; not a result of works, so that no one may boast."

1 John 5:11-12

"And this is the testimony: God has given us eternal life, and this life is in his Son. Whoever has the Son has life; whoever does not have the Son of God does not have life."

"Not a result of works, that no one may boast…" "Whoever has the Son has life…" Not exactly a moralistic diatribe.

Instead, it is Grace—The unmerited favor of the God who self-identifies as love.

I screw up all the time. I need a hero. And I see a hand extended in love, to save me.

I choose to take it…

Do You?

March 23

Glenda and I spent a couple of weeks canoeing on the Kenai Peninsula in Alaska a few years ago during salmon migration season. One thing we learned--only a live, robust salmon can swim against the current; the dead ones just drift with it. But to live, and to make sure the next generation will as well, the salmon must swim against the stream, and that takes courage.

The same with humans.

Christ said that He came that we might have life, and have it abundantly, but living life abundantly requires courage. Oh, don't get me wrong, one can drift along with the societal moirés, never making a real decision, and exist just fine, but in my opinion, the gulf between mere existence and living is as far as the gulf between living and living abundantly.

2 Timothy 1:6-7

"Therefore I remind you to stir up the gift of God which is in you through the laying on of my hands. For God has not given us a spirit of fear, but of power and of love and of a sound mind."

Power. Love. A sound mind. In Christ, those are yours for the taking. But they avail one nothing if they are not acted upon, and that takes guts.

We live in a society of convenience and rights without responsibility. Yet acting responsibly calls attention to one's self, making one stand out, and that is uncomfortable.

We live in a society that clambers for the 15-second sound bite, without the discipline to check the facts. But seeking truth obligates us to speak, even when that truth is contrary to the majority opinion, and that requires one to be brave.

Victor Hugo noted "Have courage for the great sorrows of life and patience for the small ones; and when you have laboriously accomplished your daily task, go to sleep in peace. God is awake." We have power, we have love, and we have a sound mind, but all of these require courage to actuate them. And when we have done what we can, rest, because yes, God does remain awake.

So act on the responsibilities, remembering that Christ set aside His rights.

And speak the truth, Even if your voice shakes, speak the truth.

Do these things, and you will see mountains move.

March 24

Clothes. Wearing clothes well is actually a learned skill that can take one a long way in life. I was hired to be the CFO of a large Mission board. My predecessor, we'll call him Curt Hardwater, had just been promoted to executive VP. About a year into the job I discovered a financial fraud. A seven-figure financial fraud. Perpetrated by my boss, Curt. Now, without getting into the technical legalities, he had not committed fraud to enrich himself, but to keep the "ministry" afloat financially. Well, except for his $45,000 company car, oh, and his donated, tailored Brooks Brothers suits, oh, and his all-expense-paid vacations...

I went to one of my friends in senior management to discuss the problem. Oddly, he was also named Kurt. He said something very telling. "When I came on board, I thought Curt was the model of faith and integrity. I thought he was my friend. Over the past five years, I've learned that he's just a guy who wears a suit really well." Spot on accurate, because Curt had mastered appearances, but was devoid of faith and character.

Just a guy who wears a suit really well...

1 Peter 3:3-4

"Your adornment must not be merely the external—braiding the hair, wearing gold jewelry, or putting on apparel; but it should be the hidden person of the heart, with the imperishable quality of a gentle and quiet spirit, which is precious in the sight of God."

Yes, Paul was addressing women in this verse, but it fits all of us—We can go a long way with just the adornment of looking good, but in the end, it is character that counts, true faith that counts, integrity that counts.

Depending only on external adornment is nothing more than "fake it 'till you make it." But without ever making it.

And the Church is filled with too many who excel at external adornment—especially in the "Christianese" lingo and condemnations. This is nothing more than cheap grace, and as Dietrich Bonheoffer noted, "Cheap grace is the grace we bestow on ourselves. Cheap grace is the preaching of forgiveness without requiring repentance, baptism without church discipline, Communion without confession.... Cheap grace is grace without discipleship, grace without the cross, grace without Jesus Christ, living and incarnate." Cheap grace is ineffectual. I need Christ, living and incarnate.

I need Him every day.

Oh, and I hope it is obvious that I resigned my duties at the mission board, as did the other Kurt. Curt, the guy who wore a suit really well, however, received a promotion to president.

But I can tolerate the visage looking back at me when I shave every morning.

My adornment is Christ.

March 25

In my last piece, I wrote of how, for a while, external adornment can carry a person far. The ability to wear clothes well engenders assumptions from many of competence, though, in reality, the actual substance is lacking. That piece stirred a lot of responses! One of the funniest came from our good friend, Charlotte, who wrote, "I worked with a financial services executive who 'wore a suit well.' We called him the chocolate Easter Bunny because he was hollow inside."

Ouch! Charlotte, remind me not to make you mad (though I am still laughing at the descriptor).

OK, it's true, we've all felt empty inside, as we've gone through tough times, dealt with feelings of inadequacy, you name it.

But to be hollow inside, especially when one has an appetizing exterior…

No, we were never intended to be hollow, But what then?

Romans 8:7-9

"Because the carnal mind is enmity against God; for it is not subject to the law of God, nor indeed can be. So then, those who are in the flesh cannot please God. But you are not in the flesh but in the Spirit, if indeed the Spirit of God dwells in you. Now if anyone does not have the Spirit of Christ, he is not His."

Wow! "…if indeed the Spirit of God dwells in you." Now that does not ring hollow!

And this:

Galatians 5:22-23

"But the fruit of the Spirit is love, joy, peace, longsuffering, kindness, goodness, faithfulness, gentleness, self-control. Against such there is no law.

C.S. Lewis noted, "There is a God-shaped void in every man." And we try time and again to fill that void with oh so many different things.

But the shape is never right.

But when the Spirit of God fills that void, there is fruit, specifically, love, joy, peace, longsuffering, kindness, goodness, faithfulness, gentleness, and self-control.

Not exactly a chocolate Easter bunny, eh?

All that is needed for us to realize that filling is to yield to God, to let His Spirit in.

It is the perfect shape for the void within us all.

March 26

The eyes are the windows to the soul... How true with our dogs!! Sassy's eyes bespeak utter affection. She's the one who will, throughout the day, bring me her favorite toy, just in case I might want to play with it...no matter how busy I am. Chaucer's eyes ring with trust "Daddy! Look at the WORLD!! Can you believe how BIG? Let's go explore! I know you'll keep me safe!" Maya, our rescue Great Dane who had been chained to a telephone pole and left to die, well her eyes speak of hope—"I don't want to ever leave, daddy, I HOPE this is my forever home..." And of course, the answer is yes, this is your forever home.

Inherent in each gaze is a question: "Will you play with me?" "Will you explore with me?" "Will you love me?"

And of course, the answer to each query is "yes," but they have questions and doubts, as do we, and this fact reminds me of one of my favorite passages.

Mark 9:17-27

"And one person from the crowd answered Him, "Teacher, I brought You my son, because he has a spirit that makes him unable to speak; and whenever it seizes him, it slams him to the ground, and he foams at the mouth and grinds his teeth and becomes stiff... And they brought the boy to Him. When he saw Him, the spirit immediately threw him into convulsions, and falling to the ground, he began rolling around and foaming at the mouth. And He asked his father, "How long has this been happening to him?" And he said, "From childhood. It has often thrown him both into the fire and into the water to kill him. But if You can do anything, take pity on us and help us!" But Jesus said to him, "'If You can?' All things are possible for the one who believes." Immediately the boy's father cried out and said, "I do believe; help my unbelief!" When Jesus saw that a crowd was rapidly gathering, He rebuked the unclean spirit, saying to it, "You mute and deaf spirit, I command you, come out of him and do not enter him again!" And after crying out and throwing him into terrible convulsions, it came out; and the boy became so much like a corpse that most of them said, "He is dead!" But Jesus took him by the hand and raised him, and he got up."

"I do believe; help my unbelief!" As I type this, a hot tear is running down my right cheek, for the desperation this man had for his son's welfare, and his utter honesty.

And Jesus met him in his unbelief.

I am a member of the Christian faith. I am not a member of the Christian know.

I have faith, I have hope, I have love.

And I have questions and have spent almost all of my life in pursuit of answers.

But I believe that one day, when I stand before Christ and fall at His feet in gratitude and worship, I will no longer have faith, no longer have hope, because faith and hope are anticipatory, and at that time I will know.

But I will still have love.

That is a time in eternity future. For now, eternity present, we must admit that we err when we treat Christianity as the "Christian know," and then seek to argue people to the Church by bruising them with "Evidence that Demands a Verdict" and other such nonsense.

But we do not err in loving, loving people where they are, as they are, knowing that absolute unconditional love is found in Christ, and introducing our loved ones to Him.

Christ is the safest place for us to bring our questions, our doubts, as He already knows what they are, He is just waiting for us to bring them in honesty, so He can meet us there.

Of that, I have no doubt.

March 27

I LOVE Donkeys!! Our dear friend here, Yves de Choulot runs the local Donkey rescue program (Yes, it's Mexico, and there is a Donkey rescue group!), and two of his donkeys, Hippie and Bailey, just adore Glenda and I. Hippie is a snow-white donkey, and Bailey is a grey cross-back donkey. Donkeys, usually thought of as beasts of burden, can be incredibly affectionate, and have a dog-like loyalty about them.

Ahh, the cross-back donkey...

The cross-back donkey is of a solid color, except for a darker patch of hair, starting at the shoulders, in the perfect shape of a cross. The legend goes that donkeys before the time of Christ did not have this coloration, but after a donkey's colt carried the Savior into Jerusalem, God marked the donkey with the mark of the cross, to forever remind people of the noble burden one of them once bore. This was so that anyone loading a burden on a donkey might pause to remember, and thus treat the animal with the dignity due to a creature who carried the savior.

Galatians 6:1-2

"Brothers and sisters, even if a person is caught in any wrongdoing, you who are spiritual are to restore such a person in a spirit of gentleness; each one looking to yourself, so that you are not tempted as well. Bear one another's burdens, and thereby fulfill the law of Christ."

Restoration of an individual with gentleness is a means of bearing one another's burdens, as are many other actions. And when we do this, we are fulfilling the law of Christ, which is, very simply, to love the Lord your God with all your heart, mind, soul, and strength, and to love your neighbor as yourself.

And as we bear one another's burdens, we are reminded that Christ bore our sin.

And the act of bearing one another's burdens changes us, making us more like Christ, as we act on love and empathy, even when working with those who have fallen, who have made bad choices.

To do so leaves a mark on us, on our very souls.

I think I know the shape of that mark.

March 28

Glenda and I love to snorkel, and will often work our vacation fully around that. Once we were enjoying the crystal clear waters around Curacao. We had climbed down the steep stairs from the cliff top to the ocean, slipped into the transparent water, and began to observe the beautiful reef formations and fish around us. About an hour passed, and we lifted our heads out of the water—the dock and staircase were nowhere to be seen. Oh, sure, we were still up by the cliff wall, but we were almost a mile from where we had entered, and the current was strong. Eventually, the current took us to a sliver of a beach where we could get out, and hike barefoot through the cactus-filled desert back to where we started.

Drift. Always inconvenient, oftentimes fatal.

Lesson learned—We ALWAYS lift our heads every five minutes or so now while snorkeling so we can compensate for any drift that has taken place.

And drift takes place in all areas of our lives. As one floats with any given current, cultural, emotional, political, whatever, one never feels the current, but that force can move one far from one's intended, even safe, location. The motion is subtle, unfelt, but in what seems like a blink of an eye we are seemingly irrecoverably far from where we should be, and wonder how we can ever return.

Colossians 3:1-2

"Therefore, if you have been raised with Christ, keep seeking the things that are above, where Christ is, seated at the right hand of God. Set your minds on the things that are above, not on the things that are on earth."

It is oh so easy, often pleasant even, to immerse ourselves in the things of this world, to focus on the pretty colors of material existence. All the while, we have no perception of the current, of the drift.

But it does carry us...

That is why we must lift up our eyes, and set our minds on the things above, the intangibles of Love, Faith, and so much more, so that we can be sure not to be carried away with the current, the drift.

We need to keep the Son in our eyes...

March 29

The bus from Boulder to Longmont was about half full, and I recognized the regulars. As we pulled out of the transit center, a gentleman in the back, whom I'd seen panhandling both near the university and in downtown Longmont, spoke up. "I've had the same job for just over two weeks now!" he said, his voice loud and proud. "Yesterday for the first time in my life I bought $100 worth of food. That's right, I have $100 worth of food in my refrigerator at the (name withheld) hotel. I must be the richest man in Longmont!! If anyone needs a meal, I'm cooking tonight at 6:00, room 304." I knew the name of the hotel, having driven past it often, going down one of the seedier parts of Main Street. The sign out front advertised rooms "by the hour or by the week." Yeah, that kind of place. It also had a placard on the tombstone boasting not of free HBO, but of "Free Color TV."

"Yes sir," he said again, "$100 worth of food, and I'm cooking for anyone who wants to come at 6:00 tonight." Smugly, I thought to myself that the first row of wine bottles on my wine rack was worth more than that. Then the man's words made the 18-inch hurdle from my head to my heart. He had a job now. He was no longer a beggar. He had a paycheck and used it to buy food, not drugs. And he had just invited a busload of strangers to join him at his place for dinner, the food on him.

I sniffed in deeply and tried to disguise it as a sneeze, by following up with a fake cough. Sure, I'd given the guy a dollar whenever he asked, many times over, but I had NEVER invited him to my house for dinner. And here he was, both proud and grateful for a job, and for a refrigerator full of food.

It hit me then that, though I had four advanced degrees and was finishing my Ph.D., this man was wiser at this moment than me. He intuited that gratitude and generosity had to be joined, for either to be real. A hot tear ran down my cheek, its essence an amalgam of shame for me, and utter joy for this man. Then, from my soul to my mouth came a smile, as I realized that I truly was on the bus with the richest man in Longmont, at least for that day.

2 Corinthians 9:6-8

"Remember this: Whoever sows sparingly will also reap sparingly, and whoever sows generously will also reap generously. Each of you should give what you have decided in your heart to give, not reluctantly or under compulsion, for God loves a cheerful giver. And God is able to bless you abundantly, so that in all things at all times, having all that you need, you will abound in every good work."

This is my thesis: generosity is to gratitude as an embrace is to love.

If we are truly grateful to God for what we have received, that will meet itself out in generosity, as we seek to be the Christ to others in need.

Gratitude and generosity. Both are verbs, both require action.

So whatcha doin' today?

March 30

Over the past week and a half, several people whom I care deeply about have lost loved ones, and my heart breaks for them. I especially feel for those who have been in the role of intermediate to long-term caregiver, as not only have they had to bear witness to the slow decline, but also for how their emotions are so often conflicted upon the death of their loved one.

Whereas other societies see death as a process, Americans tend to think of it as an event. As such, we tend to see only certain emotions upon the death of a loved one as appropriate. I want to make one thing very clear:

A sense of grief and a sense of relief are not in any way contradictory.

One should never feel guilt because one feels a sense of relief.

The grief portion that we feel is due to our missing a loved one, knowing that it will be a good bit of time before we can fellowship with them again.

The relief portion comes from understanding that the worst part of the dying process is over, both for our loved one, and for those who have spent so much time and effort caring for them.

Sometimes it helps to recognize when something is a process instead of an event, as it helps bring sense to the multitude of emotions we feel.

It also helps us to understand that those emotions will change through time.

Psalm 30:5

"For His anger is but for a moment, His favor is for a lifetime; Weeping may last for the night, But a shout of joy comes in the morning."

Seeing death as a process instead of as an event gives us the freedom to be honest with our emotions, and how they change through that process. It is not contradictory to be relieved that the process of sickness and dying has turned a corner. That emotion and others can exist side by side with grief, sorrow.

We built a real ofrenda this year for Dia de Muertos. As we were putting out the pictures of our loved ones, yes, I remembered the bitter tears I wept when they died. However, the photos didn't bring sadness, but a quiet sense of joy for the love these individuals had brought into my life, and when someone's love enters your life, that love sculpts the shape of your soul.

So, my friend if you have recently lost someone, realize that there is no reason to feel guilt over a sense of relief that that part of the process is over. And note that your emotions will continue to change through the process.

But this I promise: A shout of joy will come with the new morning.

March 31

My dad's house on Long Island was next door to that of Kurt Vonnegut. Now the fact that my dad never introduced me, or procured for me an autographed collection of his works has scarred me for life, but that is another story. Kurt Vonnegut, it seems was a heck of a great guy. Kurt and Joseph Heller, the author of "Catch 22," one of the best-selling books in American history, were invited to a party on Shelter Island, at the home of a hedge fund manager. Vonnegut remarked to Heller "You know, this guy literally makes more in one day than your book has in the past forty years." Heller responded, "Yeah, but I have something he never will." "What?" Vonnegut asked. "Enough," Heller replied.

Enough.

A concept so elegant, yet so elusive. We live in a society that pushes us to push for more, yet are we happy?

What is the undiscovered world called "Enough?"

Philippians 4:11-13

"Not that I speak in regard to need, for I have learned in whatever state I am, to be content: I know how to be abased, and I know how to abound. Everywhere and in all things I have learned both to be full and to be hungry, both to abound and to suffer need. I can do all things through Christ who strengthens me."

What I love here is that Paul gives no guilt trip. He knows realistically what it is to be in great need, but as an upper-class lawyer, he also understood what it was to live in abundance, but he so masterfully flips the issue back to Christ, who meets the poor where they are with hope, and reminds those in abundance that they still need the grace of God. He, then, is laying out the map to the undiscovered world of "Enough..." To keep one's focus on Christ, and understand that all true strength comes from Him.

Indeed, those periods of being in greatest need, if we face them properly, draw us oh so much closer to God. As Brennan Manning wrote, "The dominant characteristic of an authentic spiritual life is the gratitude that flows from trust—not only for all the gifts that I receive from God, but gratitude for all the suffering. Because in that purifying experience, suffering has often been the shortest path to intimacy with God."

Gratitude for the gifts, and gratitude for the suffering, both drawing us closer to God.

And in the ever-present societal pressure for us to push for more, it is so easy to forget that oftentimes we must choose to live more simply, so that others may simply live, if we, like Christ, decide to be our brothers' keeper. When we remember that 700 million people in the world are hungry, that in the United States alone, over 20% of the children in the country are food insecure—that is, they do not know if they will get another meal, then maybe, just maybe, we can see putting off that new car for another year as an act of worship, if we choose to give. That our choosing to not shop as a form of entertainment is an act of adoration to God, if we choose to give. That we are to love people and use things, as the inverse never works.

To see our acted-out love for our fellow man as our checking account, to see our actions inspired by Christ as interest earned for humanity. Oh, then, how would we build our portfolio?

Where do you choose to invest?

You made it through the first quarter! Keep on going!

Chapter Four

Thank You!

Thank you for reading! You can keep reading the Reminders of God with the Spring/Summer edition. May God fill you with the knowledge of His love.

www.ingramcontent.com/pod-product-compliance
Lightning Source LLC
Chambersburg PA
CBHW061251120726
48001CB00001B/257